LEARNING TO PLAY
WITH A LION'S TESTICLES
Unexpected Gifts From the Animals of Africa

by
Melissa J Haynes

Behler
PUBLICATIONS

California
USA

Behler Publications

Learning to Play With a Lion's Testicles
A Behler Publications Book

Copyright © 2013 by Melissa J. Haynes
Cover design by Yvonne Parks - www.pearcreative.ca.

Library of Congress Cataloging-in-Publication Data
Haynes, Melissa J.
  Learning to play with a lion's testicles : unexpected gifts from the animals of Africa / by Melissa J. Haynes.
     p. cm.
  ISBN 978-1-933016-82-5 (pbk.)
  1. Wildlife refuges--South Africa. 2. Haynes, Melissa J.--Travel--South Africa. 3. Animals--South Africa. 4. Volunteers--South Africa. 5. Grief. 6. South Africa--Description and travel. I. Title.
  SK575.S5H39 2013
  639.90968--dc23
                          2012044344

FIRST PRINTING

ISBN 13: 978-1-933016-82-5
e-book ISBN 978-1-933016-81-8

Published by Behler Publications, LLC
www.behlerpublications.com

Visit Melissa Hayne's website: http://www.melissajhaynes.com

Manufactured in the United States of America

For you, Mum

We are all connected; to each other, biologically.
To the earth, chemically.
To the rest of the universe, atomically.
~ Neil deGrasse Tyson

Table of Contents

1
Night One at the Ritz

"What was that?" Melanie's scream awakens me. Fear freezes me. We are both silent, and then I hear what she hears; something snorting and thrashing against her tent. My heart throbs as I strain to identify the sounds just inches away. What is it? A buffalo? Rhino? Lion? Elephant? Anaconda?

"Help!" Melanie shrieks.

"Stay calm. Is your backpack handy?" I try to use a soothing tone while fighting back my own fears. What's worse is that I flash back to the brownies, the little squares of heaven that I discarded just outside our tents—their scent so alluring that it has beckoned an African monster to our camp. The German journalist I convinced to spend two nights with me on a wildlife conservation project, where I will spend several weeks, is now just moments away from being eaten alive.

Melanie and I met just ten days ago on an elephant conservation project. We spent long days collecting elephant behavior data and even longer nights sharing our dreams and fears. But most of all, we shared a friendship that could only be born in a place like this, a place where life and death are only a few breaths apart and where survival is more than just instinct—it's a privilege.

Leg two of our volunteer project brought us deep within the world's most dangerous townships, where we naively believed we would be teaching HIV infected children. However, it was the children who turned out to be the teachers, and us the captivated students.

The final leg of my volunteerism journey found me on a wildlife reserve, where I'm now in the position of becoming prey to the very animals we are here to protect. And I have nothing to blame for our pending demise but my sugar addiction.

"Please help me! It's trying to get in my tent!" Melanie screams again.

"What is *it*?"

I can hear her fear dripping in every syllable. "A lion! I knew a lion would eat me if I came to this place. Why did you make me come here?"

There's nothing I can do. We have no weapons, and the closest ranger is at least a few miles away. There is no one to come to our rescue and nothing to do but prepare to fight the beast that will momentarily be ripping his way through these canvas walls. Terrified, I begin to pray. If we are to die tonight then please make it as fast and painless as possible, and please, God, forgive me for my sugar dependence.

Waiting for death to overtake us, I realize how unprepared I am. In the city, a woman is prepared for just about any emergency if she has an ample supply of chocolate, caffeine, and a good Merlot. Here in Africa, my survival kit preparation isn't much different. The key component is chocolate brownies because the only foreseen danger I could imagine out here in the middle of nowhere was a shortage of good food.

It was earlier this evening, at the welcome BBQ, when the lead ranger, a gorgeous and aloof young man named Gerrit, warned us not to keep food in our tents, saying it would attract the wildlife, or worse — bugs. Admittedly, when I first saw Gerrit, I had romantic visions of a burly ranger wrestling lions to save me, but those visions quickly evaporated when his personality proved to be non-existent. In fact, his food in the tent warning was the only thing he said all night.

I had tried to make small talk, "Can you describe the constellations for me?"

But his glazed eyes were fixated on the campfire as he sipped his beer in silence, uninterested in anything around him. The mentality in this farming area of South Africa is that women are more valuable in the home, not outside trying to do a man's job. I was prepared for some resistance to my being here, but I hadn't foreseen such blatant indifference and rudeness at my own welcome party. My ego suffered when, after many attempts, I couldn't even get as much as a polite smile from the handsome ranger. I'm not old by any stretch of the imagination, but my age falls into the latter end of the volunteer age spectrum, further adding to my feelings of alienation.

After several glasses of South Africa's finest, Melanie and I fumbled our way through the darkness to our tent camp. Gerrit's warning still ringing in my ears, I gathered the brownies from my safari survival kit. My plan was to dispose of them in the common area, but the outside blackness rendered me too afraid to make the long walk alone. Melanie was already inside her tent, and I didn't want her to know I'm afraid of the dark. What to do? I could throw the brownies from my tent, but then I'd have to try and find them in the morning to erase all the evidence. And what if a ranger finds them first? I did the only thing I could do, and left the brownies just outside of our tents.

And now the magnitude of my error is evident as the heavy canvas of Melanie's tent screeches under the claws of the beast trying to burrow through the walls.

"Oh my God!" she screams through hyperventilating gasps.

"Throw your backpack." I barely choke out the words. Earlier, Melanie said she would sleep with her backpack beside her, and if an animal encroached on her tent, she would simply throw her backpack in the opposite direction. The animal would chase the backpack thinking it was prey (as most animals have poor eyesight, relying on scent instead), and allow her enough time to escape.

"Help me!" Melanie's pleas are muffled by sobs. It's apparent she has abandoned the backpack strategy.

The volunteer placement organization said volunteering in Africa would change my life, while at the same time make an important contribution to conservation. They said I would be safe, even in the dangerous townships, and to embrace this rare and exciting experience because this was a dream many people have, but will never fulfill. They said I would be staying in a luxury tent, but the only luxurious thing about this tent is the dim camp light that keeps it from complete blackness. They also said I would see the Big Five up close, but they never mentioned I'd be left to fight them off, alone and defenseless in the middle of the night.

Suddenly outside it has become eerily quiet. "Melanie?" *Please God, let her respond.*

"Why did you make me come here?" she whimpers.

I could relay the volunteer organization's justification for giving, but it hardly seems appropriate now.

More silence follows. Collectively holding our breath, we wait to see whether the beast has moved on before we dare make any sudden movements. I try to silence the pounding of my heart. Straining my ears in search of the faintest noise outside, I'm greeted with delicious silence. Time disappears but anxiety grows. Waiting. Praying. Regretting. Questioning. Sweating. Craving. Brownies or Merlot, anything to cut the suffocating tension.

Wait, what the...?

"Is that you?" whispers Melanie.

"No. It's not you?"

The silence is replaced by monstrous snorts and repulsive grunts from the unidentified snoring beast, his comatose state likely the result of a sugar crash. At the very least, it's comforting to know that we share a love of chocolate brownies; it makes him less terrifying.

The wait for morning will be long and agonizing, giving me plenty of time to review the information collected earlier this evening from the rangers who, unlike Gerrit, have some personality and the ability to carry out a conversation. Unfortunately, the conversation focused on the smaller but deadlier creatures to be aware of on this reserve.

"Have you ever seen a puff adder?" Ranger Patrick asked.

I hadn't.

"It's the most dangerous snake on the continent, and we got lots of 'em right here."

He's proud of this fact. I, however, am not as pleased.

"Right here . . . on the reserve?"

"Yeah. They can swim, jump, and even climb trees. They are opportunistic little devils, and they're not afraid of nothin'. They got a way of getting into tiny spaces. Don't ask me how they get into those tents when the zippers are shut tight."

"They get into the tents?" As if sleeping in a tent wasn't bad enough, now I have to worry about the most dangerous snake on the continent trying to get into bed with me?

"Oh yeah. If you're lucky, you'll see one."

Lucky?

"In fact, only a few weeks ago, there was one right under that chair you're sitting on. Damn dog wouldn't stop barking at the chair. Thought he was nuts. Turns out there was a big ol' puff coiled up under there, enjoying our campfire." He laughed.

I had the sudden urge to jump from the chair, screaming.

"They got a big thick, square head like a bull, and the attitude of a bull, too, nasty little bastards."

"Are they deadly?"

"Pretty much. A puff's venom will kill a person in thirty-five minutes. It's a rough thirty-five minutes."

"My God . . . " Shock and fear steal my breath away. I'd never even heard of this type of snake before, and now they tell me these venomous monsters not only sneak into tents, but also can kill a person after a half-hour of excruciating torture? What the hell am I doing here?

"But there's good news."

"What's that?" Please say they're incredibly rare, or that they're as aloof and uninterested in women as Gerrit is.

"The hospital is only thirty minutes away. No one's died here yet." All the rangers except for Gerrit sniggered when he said that. "We've had a few injuries here, but no fatalities," he said through a wide smile. "And everyone has gone on to lead normal lives for the most part once they leave here."

"For the most part...?"

"Once there was a volunteer who climbed a tree to cut branches for the ellies. Reckoned he was pretty good with a machete, and he was. But he lost his footing and landed spread eagle on a freshly hacked branch."

"Ouch."

"Yeah, cut his scrotum clean open from one end to the other."

"Oh my . . ."

"He passed out before we even loaded him into the back of the truck. He slept the whole way to the hospital. They stitched him up good. Could have been worse, could have cut his own balls off with his machete when he fell."

All the rangers broke out into a rolling laughter. I wondered how many volunteers had accidently cut off their fingers, toes, or other appendages.

"There's some nasty spiders in these parts, too, but their venom can't kill you."

"What kind of spiders?"

"Oh, there are lots here, too many to mention. The venom only kills the flesh, turns it black. But as long as we cut it out before it spreads to vital organs, you're fine."

"Cut what out?"

"The flesh. We've all been trained to do that."

The rangers broke out in laughter again. I dared not even look at Melanie, who was terrified to come here in the first place. Learning about climbing snakes that sneak into tents and flesh-killing spiders would be enough to send her running to Cape Town. I give her kudos for staying in her chair. After all, she came here because of me. My reasons for being here have wholly different origins.

There is nothing quite like an African sky. The famous hues of an African sunrise render most speechless, but an African sky at night is just as remarkable and tonight's sky is no exception. At its center is the Milky Way, a dazzling rainbow of diamonds that stretches from the western horizon to the east, where it disappears into oblivion. The rest of the sky is black, an endless pit of dark velvet that leaves me feeling insignificant. But once I adjust to the darkness, I realize I'm not insignificant, but connected, like the trillions of individual stars above that together form huge clouds of galactic dust.

We are symbiotic beings, although we are mostly oblivious that others subsist and rely on us for protection, conservation, and ultimately, for survival. Distant countries, endangered species, and struggling societies—they are like the stars above and in the daily hustle of our busy lives, we forget they exist. It is only when the darkness in our own lives becomes so overwhelming that we search for the comfort that comes from something or someone outside of ourselves to fill the void that loneliness brings.

We search for greater meaning and purpose when hopelessness and fear become too great. It is in searching that we will find that which gives us hope, like the glowing star that suddenly becomes apparent when searched for in an outwardly black sky.

But on this night, inside my tent, in the silence, staring into the blackness, I have never felt so alone. The shock of past events creep into the dark space of my soul, filling it with memories I am trying to leave behind, memories I cannot escape, even here in an insignificant tiny tent camp in the middle of Africa. It has been two years, but the conversation replays in my mind as though it happened earlier today.

~~~

"I can't move," my mother's distressed voice is barely audible on the other end of the telephone. She wastes no breath by saying hello.

"What's wrong?" I ask, trying to wake up.

"I had a glass of wine."

"A glass of wine?"

"Maybe I had three or four, I don't remember."

I am still half asleep and unsure of what my response should be. After all, as of late, wine has become her best friend, her loyal companion, and one she refuses to let go of despite how bad it is for her and how much I beg her to.

"And I took morphine, too."

This last piece of information jolts me into full alertness because she has never mixed alcohol and narcotics before.

"I'm on my way." I hang up the phone without waiting for a reply.

The normally twenty-minute drive takes seven minutes in the light midnight traffic. When I enter her house I find her lying on the living room floor, a blank stare covers her vacant eyes, and dried tears have left stains on her cheeks. I fear the worst.

"Mum?" I whisper.

"I have to go to the bathroom, but I can't move. Please help me." She begins to cry.

She looks embarrassed and frail. It's hard to believe this is the woman who had the tenacity of a bull and whom everyone feared—even my father. She was a woman who never backed away from a challenge and feared nothing. Looking at her now, she looks helpless, weak, and vulnerable. I don't know this woman.

I try to lift her. It is impossible. Her body is dead weight. "I need to get help."

"Please don't. I don't want anyone to see me like this." She turns her head away in shame.

"I can't move you by myself."

"Just drag me."

I grip her wrists tightly and begin to drag her across the hardwood floor, but once we reach the carpet, her body refuses to move. "Bring me something," she pleads. "A pad, some paper towel, anything. I have to pee so badly."

I run upstairs searching for something. In the spare room I find some baby diapers and bring them to her. Pulling one apart, I try to protect her dignity by acting as though this is all normal. I place it underneath of her. She relieves herself and feels her own dignity slipping away. Over the next several hours she has to relieve herself many times. She tries in vain to hold the diaper underneath her, but her arms refuse to move, and each time she becomes more frustrated and ashamed.

My own exhaustion and ignorance of what she is experiencing turns into aggravation. The resentment I feel towards her makes me feel like a monster. I am helpless. There is nothing I can do to stop this train that is about to end in a horrific crash. She is relying on me to save her, but I can't, and with that admission, a magnitude of guilt comes crashing down all around me.

I make a panicked call to her doctor, and he says it's time to bring her in. It is five days before Christmas. I can't move her, and even if I could, she wouldn't go. He solves the problem by sending a non-emergency ambulance for her. All I have to do is keep her comfortable until they arrive within the next few hours.

Eventually mental exhaustion sets in and I lay beside her on the floor. I am unable to sleep with the rush of fears racing through my mind as reality sets in.

She, too, is wide-awake. I wait for her to speak, to say something, anything, but the silence thickens between us like a brick wall as it always has.

"I have cancer." It was only a few months ago she was diagnosed. In that second, life changed forever. It would never go back to the way it was. Regret strangled me as I repeated her words. There were so many things I hadn't said, so many things I hadn't done. I thought there was time. I thought she would always be there, she was my mother, she had to always be there. She will outlive everyone one of us, we use to say. She was untouchable, or so I thought.

"I'm sorry I wasn't a good mother," she finally whispers.

"Please don't say that." I try not to cry myself as I wipe her tears away with a tissue.

"I'll never be back at this house again." Her words are heavy with sadness.

"Yes you will." I try to steady my voice, but deep down I know she is probably right.

This time the monster is devouring not only her strength, but mine, too. It is relentless, and I have never hated it more than I hate it right now, for I finally realize I have no control over this disease that already killed my father and is now killing her.

Cancer isn't just a monster; it is an epidemic that no weapon, poison, or even an army can destroy. One never thinks it will invade their family, and that is exactly when it strikes. I didn't think evil could be this ruthless but it is, and its torturous rampage has just begun. Soon, it will take not only a life, but my innocence too.

"I'm scared, I'm so very scared. Please protect me."

"I will always protect you, Mum."

"I feel so alone. Can you hold my hand?"

"I'm already holding your hand."

I wait until early morning to call an ambulance to see if she will regain muscle control, but she hasn't. She is getting worse. Her hand has become cold and transparent as the blood has long since stopped circulating through it. I squeeze it hard trying to draw the life back into it while praying for the sound of sirens.

Back on the game reserve in Africa the contents of my safari survival kit have proven to be life-saving after all. The chocolate brownies satisfied the beast's appetite for fattening treats; morning is here, and Melanie and I are still alive. We never did see the wild animal that ravaged our tent camp and kept us awake all night with its snores, and for that we are grateful.

Melanie says she left her light on all night. She asks me if I slept with mine on, I tell her I didn't. My secret is safe because our heavy canvas tents block all incoming and outgoing light.

"You are so brave!" she exclaims.

I can never admit that I too was terrified and slept with my light on. I must at least appear to be fearless; after all, it's no good if the two of us are afraid.

I'm confident that the rest of my nights at "the Ritz" will be much less eventful now that I know not to bring food into the tent camp.

2
Mud Bath

Neither of us slept much last night, and what little we did get was shattered with the wretched screech of the Hadeeda at sunrise passing over our tent camp. It's not like this is some giant bird, in fact it's not much bigger than a seagull. It's white with petrol sheen-covered wings and a long curved beak. The call of the Hadeeda is unmistakable, and some say it can even wake the dead. I believe it. Thankfully, there are no other birds on earth that share their high-pitched squawks. When they fly, it sounds like they're saying "Oh my Gawd, my Gaaaawwddd, Gaaaawwwdddd, Gawwwwwwwddddd," with each shriek higher, longer, and louder than the last. The locals claim it's due to their fear of heights.

They are supposedly a close relative of the Egyptian Ibis that are often depicted on ancient temple walls. However, I can easily claim that there is nothing sacred or worship-worthy of these birds' shrieks.

After our rude awakening, we have a simple breakfast of porridge and instant coffee in the common area that lies on the edge of our tent camp. It has a basic kitchen, a few lounge chairs and a shelf full of field guides. We eat quickly, expecting a ranger to arrive at any moment and whisk us away on a great adventure. Maybe we'll learn how to dart wildlife, wrestle crocs, or herd elephants. The possibilities are endless. But no one shows up. With a quickening, pace we circle the perimeter of our tent camp, trying to get a glimpse of what lay beyond its borders. Our search is fruitless, nothing but a bored buffalo and some scrub brush. We take some pictures, do several more laps around the camp and re-organize our tents. Still no one shows up.

By this time the sun is high, and it's too hot to stay in our tents, so we drag our sleeping bags out in the sun, next to a large mud pit in the middle of our camp. Melanie is journaling, and I'm searching the horizon for any sign of a ranger. Nothing. I'm hot and as bored as the buffalo watching us, so I get the brilliant idea to take a dip in the mud pit.

The cool mud squishes in between my toes with a delightful *shlop*. I pull my foot out and cautiously step forward. A sudden jolt forces my leg deeper into the black mud and it disappears below the knee.

"What the hell are you doing, woman?" A loud voice bellows across our quiet little tent camp disrupting our lazy Sunday morning.

"I said, what the hell are you doing?" The voice comes at me again, this time louder and angrier. I try to turn around to see who is yelling at whom,

"Don't move! If you move, you're dead." His tone reeks of rage.

This time I recognize the voice. It is that of the lead ranger, Gerrit, my boss for the next several weeks. The first time I saw him, he nearly took my breath away. Out here in the vastness, one could easily get lost in his deep green eyes, or be distracted by the brown locks of soft curls that dance around his neck. But unfortunately, he doesn't have a personality to match his good looks. Instead, he is rude, and getting ruder by the second.

My legs sink deeper into the mud pit.

"Why are you yelling at me?" I shout back, as Gerrit runs toward me.

He skids to a stop and yanks me out of the mud with such force, he nearly dislocates my shoulder. His piercing green eyes are lit up, and a Y-shaped vein bulges in the center of his forehead.

"You city women are the stupidest species on this earth!"

Where does this Neanderthal get off insulting me? "How dare you talk to me like that!"

"You think you can come to Africa and do stupid things. You think you're untouchable, and when you screw up you think someone will always be there to save you!"

"Save *me*? From what? The mud?"'

"Do you not see that?" His finger stabs at the far bank of the mud pit.

There, lying perfectly camouflaged, with only his yellow eyes and fang-lined jaws visible, is a king crocodile. My knees instantly turn to jelly, and my stomach hardens into a tight ball. Melanie's mouth drops at the same time her pen hits the ground. Had I taken my usual approach of running and jumping into the water, I would already be in the death roll embrace of a crocodile.

Gerrit's face turns deeper purple with every word he shouts. "You watch too much TV in America, you think a safari is romantic. People die every single day and it's people like me who die trying to save intolerable people like you. You come here under the premise of 'volunteering,' but you just end up wasting my time because I am the one who has to save *your* ass from your own stupidity!"

"Save my ass? *Save my ass?* Are you kidding me?" The words squeeze out through gritted teeth, and I can feel the blood pulsing in my temples. Granted, wading in a mud pit in Africa may not have been the wisest move, but had he actually shown up on time, I wouldn't have gone in the pit in the first place. Jerk.

"If I was in my right mind I would strip my mood on you!"

"*Strip my mood?* What the hell does that mean?" I demanded. Obviously, he is a lunatic.

"It means you're an ignorant city woman who couldn't survive a day in the bush if your life depended on it. I've had it with people like you coming here wasting my time, my resources, and most of all, my patience. You think you can play with a lion's testicles with no recourse." The words shoot out of his mouth like nails from a nail gun.

"Play with a lion's testicles? What kind of a sick pervert are you?" It is no longer a hunch he is crazy, it's confirmed. "And hold on a minute. Melanie and I were almost killed last night because of *you!*"

"What are you babbling about, woman?"

"There was a wild animal in our camp. I think it was a lion, but it may have been a rhinoceros, it was hard to distinguish but it was here and it tried to kill us."

"Don't be ridiculous, if a lion wanted to kill you, you'd be dead."

"Well, something was there, and you left us alone and defenseless. We didn't even have a weapon to protect ourselves. We're lucky to be alive, no thanks to you. It was my own survival kit that saved us!"

"What survival kit?" Melanie asks with a small squeak.

Up until now she had been speechless, instead watching the crocodile for any sudden movement. I hadn't told her about the brownies I had to discard outside our tents, and I wasn't about to now.

Gerrit stomps off towards our tents. When he gets there he begins poking at the ground, picking up blades of grass and tossing them aside. "It appears your lion is very rare indeed," he finally says.

"My God! A lion! It was a lion in our camp?" Melanie gasps, "I cannot spend another night here, I want to go to Cape Town today." Her face is ghostly white, and she looks as though she may pass out.

"I knew it!" I yelled, shaking a muddy finger in his face. "I can't believe we're still alive. This is *your* fault for leaving us alone without a weapon. It's by the sheer grace of God and our survival skills that we're alive today." I put my hands on my hips, squaring off for a verbal duel. "So what was it? A rare, gigantic, man-eating lion?"

"NO!" His teeth are clenched so tightly his jaw muscles are pulsing. "Your lion is rare because it is the only lion in the world that has quills!" He holds up a long, sharp quill as evidence.

"Quills?" I lean forward for a closer look.

"Yes, quills. Your lion was not a lion at all. It was a porcupine, a scavenger, an African rat. You had food in your tent, didn't you?" His eyes pierce through me as he throws the quill past me, narrowly missing me.

"Of course not." Defiance conceals my guilt.

"Well, they only come in here if they smell food, so unless someone else laced your camp with food, it had to have been you."

"So maybe it wasn't a lion, but we could just as easily have been shot by that porcupine. Stabbed in the eye, blinded for life. I've read of that happening to people."

"Porcupines don't shoot their quills. They back into their enemy and poke them."

"Well, we could have been injured if the porcupine did that."

"It would only back into you if you were chasing it. Would you chase a two-hundred pound African porcupine in the middle of the night?"

A red flush creeps across my cheeks. Looking away, I pull my hair forward over my reddening ears. Leaping into that mud pit with a waiting croc would be less painful than this. I quickly change the subject. "Anyway, Melanie and I are bored. We want to do something, can we at least go for a walk?"

"No. You can't leave the camp. You won't last five minutes out there before something eats you."

We'll die of boredom if we have to spend another minute in this tent camp. "Can we work today? We want to do something. Anything. "

"It's Sunday, no one works on Sundays in Africa."

"What are we supposed to do, then?"

"Relax, take the day off. We'll get that croc moved and maybe later we'll take Melanie on a game drive because she's leaving tomorrow morning."

"And me, too?"

"Yes, it would probably be best if you left tomorrow morning as well. You haven't even started work and you've already disrupted the camp."

"I meant the game drive. Can I go on the game drive, too?"

He sighed heavily. "As long as you stay in your seat, away from the wildlife . . . and me."

3

Getting Acquainted

Ranger Gerrit pulls up to the tent camp in a rickety old white pick-up truck. The white paint is sparse and the carriage appears to lean to the left under the weight of a broken axle. It doesn't look anything like the safari game drive vehicles one may expect to see on a game reserve. It looks like something that belongs in a scrap yard.

I step inside, careful where I place my feet, since rust has eaten through most of the floor, leaving behind gaping holes the size of apples. There are no handles for the windows, so they are permanently half-open, rain or shine. The door doesn't close properly, either, and it takes several attempts before it stays partially shut. Melanie takes special care not to lean against the door, since it will open under the slightest pressure. Predictably, there is no stereo, just basic functions on the dashboard, which Gerrit says not to touch because none of them work. Satisfied, he has given us a proper introduction to this piece of twisted scrap metal that we're stuffed into like sardines, he chirps out a "Right, let's go."

We are beyond underwhelmed, and even he can sense it.

"This is Harrison," he says with obvious affection.

"It has a name?" It's hard to believe he can conjure up affection for anything, let alone this ugly and worthless hunk of junk.

"Yes, I just told you, we call him Harrison."

"Why Harrison?"

"You will soon learn why," he chuckles. "And don't let looks deceive you, Harrison is a mighty warrior."

With that he pulls the stick into reverse and, with a loud huuccccckkkk, Harrison rolls backwards. He shifts into first and again, Harrison coughs a long huuuccckkkk. Melanie and I cringe and cover our ears. How can it be possible that this rusty hulk sounds worse than it looks? "Is Harrison going to make it?"

"Harrison is a champion," he answers confidently while accelerating towards the gate.

The electric gate slowly opens, revealing more of the reserve with each inch. We have not yet explored the reserve, being bound by the tent camp and common area up until now. Finally, the gate opens fully and we chug forward around a slight bend in the pitted road.

There are no other signs of human life for as far as the eye can see. There are no buildings, no traffic, no streets and no congestion—only God's landscaping. The reserve is cut into a valley at the base of the Landberg mountain range. The mountains stand tall and still like soldiers clad in dark blue uniforms, topped in white fur caps, guarding this kingdom of paradise that has been held hostage by drought for more than a hundred years. Snow covers the peaks in the African winter, teasing the dry, parched valley below, where it will never reach.

The valley is covered in golden grass and spotted with baobab and gum trees imported from Australia. A few Jurassic Park-sized aloe plants scatter the landscape, whose winter flowers are now in full bloom, and resemble red, orange, and yellow fire pokers. The wind dances through the fynbos and thatch reeds, playing tricks on my eyes, so they look like big cats.

The abundance of blue sky stretches far beyond my sight, and is as endless as last night's black sky, going on without boundaries. The African sun's rays stretch over the mountain range and tickle my face, warming it instantly. Moments ago, we were trapped in a tiny tent camp, now we are living within the pages of a *National Geographic* magazine that has sprung to life. There is a sense of openness, timelessness, and peacefulness that fills this valley. No thoughts of yesterday or tomorrow—only this moment, so far away from everything.

In the distance, I see two gigantic elephants. "Look over there, Melanie," I whisper, "ellies!"

"Oh my! How cute! Look how that one is standing over the other one. How adorable." Melanie begins snapping photos with her expensive journalist's camera.

"Those ellies are not cute or adorable. They're killers," Gerrit grunts.

"Killers?"

"Killers. They killed a rhino just last month."

"Why?"

"Could be an on-going turf war, or maybe it's just because those ellies are plain mean."

"They're mean? I didn't think ellies were mean-natured."

"These don't like people or anyone else, for that matter, except Shaka. They don't try and kill him, but they won't let anyone else in their camp."

"Who's Shaka?" I ask.

"Shaka's an Eland. He was hand-reared. He's as big as a horse now and has horns over a foot long, but he still thinks he's a baby. If we release him onto the reserve, the wild Elands won't accept him, and a cat will eventually get him, so he lives here with the ellies. He's always breaking into the tent camp or the common area to steal food. So if you see him, remember that he's harmless."

Too bad he didn't steal those brownies out of my tent before bedtime last night.

"Where did the elephants come from?"

"They were brought here from a training camp. They were trying to train them to be safari tour guides so tourists could ride into the bush, but they'd have no part of it. Every time a human got on their back they'd throw him off and try to trample him to death."

"So why are they here?"

"It was a matter of finding a place to retire, or be culled, so the reserve stepped in and offered to take them. The male's name is Selati, he's the one on the ground. The female is Kittibon, she's the one standing over him. She's the most aggressive, meanest ellie we've ever seen, and she especially hates women."

"As much as you do?" I whisper under my breath.

"What?"

"Nothing."

"How did they kill the rhino?" I ask. "Don't these electrical fences keep them separated?"

"Oh no, no, no, no" he scoffs, "these fences are just a mental block to the wildlife. They can get through them quite easily. The ellies and rhinos are always pulling them down." To punctuate the point, he waves in the direction of our tent camp.

"You mean that fence? The fence around our tent camp?" Surely he wasn't pointing at our tent camp, was he?

"Yes."

"So, does that mean they have to go through our tent camp to fight each other?"

"Yes."

"Doesn't that put us in a slightly precarious position?"

Gerrit goes quiet again, his stare fixed on the horizon.

"Hello?" Am I the only one who sees the insanity in this?

"We're treating the male rhino for aggression, it seems to be working. There haven't been any battles lately. It's a new drug hormone therapy. I believe in your part of the world it is quite common to treat the woes of women with hormones." He begins to laugh.

"Funny. What about the lions on the other side of our camp? Will they run through an electric fence, too?"

"The lions won't pull down a fence," he reassures me.

"Thank God." My whole body relaxes, and Melanie and I share a relieved smile.

"They'll jump over it."

I wait for him to laugh, or to say "ha ha, just kidding," but he does neither. I feel Melanie stiffen beside me, and decide it's best to no longer discuss the ease of accessibility these animals have to our tent camp.

"What does the name Kittibon mean?"

"Kittibon is Xhosa for 'I have seen.' Elephants are intelligent, social animals. They're emotional. They get attached to one another in life, and even through death. They bury each other's remains and visit the graves of their loved ones the way humans do. They don't forget each other, or events. Kittibon was orphaned very young when her herd was killed by poachers. She was the only elephant who survived. They found her surrounded by dozens of mutilated ellies with their tusks cut out."

"That's terrible, the poor elephant."

"Yeah, that's why she hates humans, and no one can get close to her except Harrison."

"Harrison the truck?"

"No, Harrison the elephant groom. He lives in the elephant stable with them. You'll meet him later today."

"And what does Selati mean?" I ask.

"Selati is Xhosa for sugar. Selati is sweet like sugar, he is gentle, except when Kittibon gets aggressive, then he fights alongside her. But he doesn't hate people the way she does."

"Why do they need a stable to sleep in? Elephants don't sleep indoors in the wild."

"They were both orphaned young. Selati was found in a farmer's field. No one knows his story, but poachers probably killed his herd, too. They are creatures of habit now. They come in at 5 o'clock and know there will be food, branches, and fresh water waiting for them. If things aren't just the way they like them, they will let us know in a hurry by breaking a pillar or kicking down their stable walls. We've rebuilt the stable twice already. As long as we keep the ellies happy, they won't try and kill us."

Holding up my camera I ask, "Can we get a little closer to take some pictures?"

"Later, when they're in the stable. It's not safe to go into the elephant camp when they're out in the open. They charge trucks and try to attack them . . . probably reminds them of poachers."

We continue down a long bumpy road pitted with large stones and potholes so big a small car could be swallowed whole by one. The door swings open many times, forcing Melanie to hold it shut with one arm. I keep an arm around her shoulders to keep her from rolling out.

Finally we arrive at the star attraction of the reserve; the lion camp. The first gate opens slowly and Harrison edges forward and waits until it closes before the next gate opens even slower in front of us. Melanie's body stiffens and she leans in closer to me, pulling the door with her. Her arms are rigid and covered in goose bumps. The lion camp is more than a hundred acres; nothing lives in this camp except for the lions. I search the tall grass, anxious to see the giant predators, but find nothing.

"Where are they?" I whisper.

"Don't worry, they'll soon find us," says Gerrit.

Harrison pushes along the perimeter road. My foot drums uncontrollably on the broken floorboards. It is quickly muted by the beat of my heart pounding against my chest. Soon we are on the border of our tent camp, and it becomes very real just how close we are sleeping to these killer cats.

"How did the lions come to be at the reserve?" Melanie asks.

"They were being raised as trophy lions for sport hunting. Not fair really, when you think about it. Tourist pays thousands of dollars to 'hunt' a lion in an enclosed space; lion doesn't stand a chance because he's in an oversized trap. Tourist thinks he's just conquered the most dangerous predatory cat in Africa, but he hasn't hunted anything. He's just killed an animal that was trapped in a box with nowhere to run anyway. Where's the skill or sport in that?"

"Does that really still happen?"

"Yeah, lots of money in it for the greedy breeders. But these lions got lucky. We rescued them before they could be hunted. But they'll never be normal lions because they've never hunted for themselves. They've always been fed by humans, humans wanting to fatten them up for the game."

"So are they tame lions then?" Melanie's tone is momentarily hopeful.

"On the contrary. These lions are more dangerous than lions in the wild because they don't fear humans. In fact, they don't fear anything. And what's worse, is these lions associate humans with food because we feed them. Wild lions fear humans, and they'll usually just run away if they smell us. But not these lions. These lions are killing machines. One time, we let them go on the reserve to see if their natural instincts would kick in and they would hunt for themselves. They hunted all right. They killed everything with a pulse—only not to eat, just for sport."

Up ahead on the side of the hill I notice three massive objects that look like tombstones. "What are those?"

"Those are the lions," Gerrit beams.

As soon as he says it the tombstones stand up, doubling in size. They are larger than I could have ever imagined a lion could be. I can see the massive cats' bulging muscles even from this far away. Their presence is daunting.

"Have you ever seen a lion rip the spine out of a fleeing zebra?" Gerrit asks.

"Uh no, can't say I have." Thank God.

"Well that lioness right there did exactly that . . . with one claw, she swatted that zebra like a fly and pulled his spine clean out of him." With a gleam in his eye, a satisfied smile smears across his face.

If she could do that to a zebra, what would she do to a human?

"Hold on!" Gerrit suddenly shouts.

Hold on to what? There is nothing to hold onto in this piece of crap except for Melanie, who is already holding on to me for dear life. Harrison takes off with a loud huuucckkkkkk as Gerrit jams it into third gear and plunges over the hill, sending Harrison into a downward dive bomb. Melanie and I hook our feet into the rusted out holes for fear of rolling out the handicap door.

At the bottom of the hill, Gerrit stops the truck abruptly and looks over his shoulder. I peer into the rear view mirror. Flying down the hill, at full speed, is a cloud of blonde fur, muscle, and fangs. Why the hell is he stopping? Oh my God, this is it. He really does hate women; he's brought us here to feed us to the lions. We should have stayed in the damn tent camp. The cats are upon us, circling, panting, and glaring at the ignorant city women.

"My window won't close," Melanie breathes.

"Shhhhh, be quiet and don't be afraid," Gerrit whispers. "Predators can smell fear, it's an aphrodisiac to them, makes them excited and want you even more."

"Seriously?"

"Yes, it's true. All animals can smell weakness, even humans can, but wild animals have honed the skill because they rely on it for survival."

There is a distinct tremor in Melanie's voice. "How can I not be afraid when there is a lion looking at me, licking its lips?"

"Just stay calm, they think we have food. Once they see we don't have anything in the back, they'll back off."

Aren't we food?

There are three lions, one male and two lionesses. The male is almost as tall and long as Harrison, and his head nearly as wide as the cab.

"Don't make eye contact either," Gerrit whispers.

I quickly turn my eyes away to see Melanie who is now paler than Harrison's white paint. She has one hand dug into my knee, the other on the door handle. Her knuckles are so white it looks like they are about to break through her skin.

The larger of the two lionesses, the reigning one, comes forward slowly, but with confidence. Her eyes narrow as she focuses on the back of the truck, coming closer and closer. When will she stop? I glance over at the half-open window, quickly calculating if she can fit one of her solid arms through— the answer is undeniable; hell yes, she can.

Melanie's eyes are fixed straight ahead, she is too afraid to look. Mine are on the lioness. Her prowess is mesmerizing, I can't pull away. She moves forward past the back of the truck and slithers up to Melanie's window. She is only five feet away—one stride for a lion. Melanie's hand tightens on my knee, and I try not to wince as her nails dig in. I look past the lioness, trying not to make eye contact, but her glare is magnetic. She examines the inside of the cab, sizing up each one of us, calculating the risk-benefit of smashing through the window.

"Please take me out of here. I beg of you, please," Melanie whimpers.

I can feel her fear. She is petrified, more petrified than I have ever seen anyone. Gerrit is already turning over the engine, bypassing first gear he jams it straight into second, pounding the accelerator into the floor. Harrison hucccckkkks and chucks, but takes off without hesitation. The lioness follows, giving chase. She keeps up beside Melanie's window for a good two minutes—or as Melanie would later describe, two hours.

We are both relieved when the first gate closes behind us on the way out of the lion camp. My knee, however, will take a little longer to recover from Melanie's nails.

Harrison rolls up to the front door of the elephant stable and stops with a sigh. Inside, the ellies have returned for the night and will be eating.

"When we go in, don't make eye contact with the ellies," Gerrit orders. "And don't try and touch them. Just observe,"

"Is it safe to go in there?" Melanie asks.

"Relatively safe. They're behind concrete-reinforced wood pillars as thick as tree trunks, but that hasn't stopped them before." Gerrit lets out a sinister chuckle.

"I think I'll wait outside," says Melanie. The visit to the lion camp has left her shaken.

"It's fine. They're eating now so they won't care if we're there. Come in, Melanie."

We cautiously enter the stable and stop just inside the door. Not ten feet in front of us are two massive prehistoric wrinkled giants. The light is dim, but I can see Kittibon looking at us through the pillars. The sound of snapping branches fills the air as they effortlessly break them with their powerful trunks. The stench is nearly unbearable; a mixture of urine, dung, and something unrecognizable — perhaps it's just the stink of elephants.

"*Hhhhhhuuuuuuuuuuukkkkkkkkk hhhhhhhhhhuuuuuuuuukkkkkk*"

Melanie grabs my arm as we both take a step backwards at the putrid noise. These elephants not only stink, they make repulsive sounds.

"*Hhhhhhuuuuuuuukkkkkkkkk*"

It is the disgusting long drawl of a hork; one that comes from deep within the throat, collecting strands of mucous along its way up.

"*Huk, huk, huk, huk*"

The final clucking sounds are almost too much for my stomach, as strays are snatched from the nasal passage and drawn down deep into the throat. Vile and putrid as it is, Gerrit ignores the sound, no doubt use to it.

A few minutes later, it comes again, like the horrific aftershocks of an earthquake, a virtual anarchism in my ears. "That is disgusting," I finally declare. Does no one else hear it?

"What is?" asks Gerrit.

"That hideous racket those elephants are making, it's making me ill."

"That's not the ellies," he says, laughing, "that's Harrison."

"Harrison?"

"Yes, Harrison the elephant groom, the one we named the truck after."

Now it makes sense. Harrison the truck's faulty transmission sounds just like Harrison the elephant groom's disgusting habit.

"Where is he?"

"He's in his room, over there." Gerrit points to the rear corner. Behind tall stacks of bundled Lucerne is a poorly made structure of thin walls.

"He *lives* in there?" 'How could any person actually live amongst this stink?

"Yes, he has a bathroom, bed, and satellite TV. He's on holidays now, but isn't going anywhere. He took two weeks off to watch the World Cup. You won't see him, nothing will drag him away from the telly, but you'll definitely hear him." He roars with laughter this time.

Gerrit shouldn't be laughing. He isn't much better than Harrison himself. He has the annoying habit of placing a small 'huuckk' in the middle of all his sentences. I'm about to mention this to him when something catches my eye. It's Kittibon. She stretches her trunk towards us and, like a vacuum hose, inhales our scent. I freeze, not even allowing my breath to stir. She withdraws her trunk. It appears we are safe. I slowly and carefully lean forward to get a better look at this magnificent creature before us.

KABAM.

My scream fills the tiny stable.

The cow whipped a trunk full of sawdust in my face. It hurts like hell. It's in my eyes, my mouth, which is still gaping open in shock, even up my nose—filthy elephant! All I can taste is the salty essence of what can only be elephant piss and dung.

Before I can retreat, she hits me with yet another missile of dung-encrusted sawdust. I spit it out and wipe it out of my eyes, I can't believe it. I just cannot believe it.

"Hahahahahahahahaha! That is ayoba!" Gerrit is in hysterics. Even Melanie is barely able to contain her laughter.

"It's not funny, that hurt. That cow just assaulted me!" I shriek.

"I told you she doesn't like people," Gerrit howls. "Now she has shown you her boundaries . . . and who's boss around here."

"Horrible elephant!"

Kittibon raises her trunk again, and I quickly hide behind Melanie, who is no longer trying to contain her laughter; she is all but rolling on the ground.

"Maybe you should go to Cape Town tomorrow with Melanie," Gerrit says.

"Why?"

"Don't you feel like you've experienced a Big Five Reserve enough already? You've seen all the Big Five today, and you've slept in a tent. From here on in it's nothing but long days of hard work and even longer nights alone in your tent camp."

This Neanderthal won't quit. I should follow Kittibon's cue and slap him in the face with some dung. Does he actually think he can scare me away? "'I'm not afraid to work hard."

"You've never worked on a game reserve. It's tough physical labor."

"Let me guess, too tough for a city woman?"

"I didn't say that, but it is hard work, and we can't slow down our operations for a volunteer."

"I don't expect you to." *This guy really is clueless. Did I show up here in heels and a mini skirt? Hell no. I came here with one intention only; to work, and I'm a damn hard worker. Give me some credit, you moron.*

"And once Melanie leaves, you will be all alone in the tent camp. There's nothing to entertain you at night."

"I don't need to be entertained. I'm self-sufficient. I have books to read, and I'm not afraid."

Liar. I am a liar. I am terrified to sleep in that tent camp alone, in the dark, without a weapon, or German-speaking decoy.

"Well, it's not too late; you have until the morning to decide," Gerrit says. "Now, watch this . . ." His voice is stern when he shouts at the ellies. "Shake!"

At the same time, both ellies shake their heads from side to side. Kittibon barely shakes hers but Selati is shaking his eagerly, like a dog trying to please his master. Gerrit throws them each an apple. Showoff.

4

Sentenced

When we exit the stable, I notice two animals in the distance, inside the elephant camp. "What kind of animals are those?"

"Those are inmates," Gerrit says.

"Inmates?"

"Yes, inmates. The one on the left is a bontebok, and the other is a wildebeest. They kept killing off members of their herds, so they've been sentenced to the ellie camp."

"How come they don't try to kill each other?" Melanie asks.

"Beats me," he says with a shrug.

Both of these lost souls have rap sheets speckled with violence, aggression, and murder. The bontebok killed at least three other bonteboks, and the wildebeest killed two members of his clan. They haven't yet come up with a suitable hormone therapy for bonteboks and wildebeests. Only rhinoceroses are so fortunate.

Back inside the fence line of our tiny tent camp, I observe the two inmates for nearly an hour. They don't do much. Occasionally, they kick around, but soon stop when they realize there's no point. No one's watching, heck, no one even knows or cares that they're here. There is no one to talk to, no one to play with, no females to impress, and no one to frolic with. There's not even anyone to battle with because a battle with an ellie would be tantamount to suicide. They are all alone.

They stand and wait, searching, but nothing changes, no one is coming to see them. They seem lost, resigned to insignificance in solitary confinement. They don't look like killers. Do they wonder if they'll ever be reunited with their herds? After all, what are they if they don't have a herd?

"Hello! I am over here! Do you see me? I see you. I am your neighbor. Come over here!" The bontebok tilts his head, but doesn't come any closer.

The first thing to do is give them names. The bontebok is easy to name, he will be Bonty from now on. Not just for the obvious reason, but because he just looks like a Bonty. He's mostly brown, but has knee-high white socks (think roller-skating disco retro look), a cute white bottom that looks like he's wearing matching short shorts, and a broad white stripe down the center of his face, all rounded out by little satellite dishes for ears and black horns that curve outwards just at the top. Come to think of it, he could even pass for a Monty, but Bonty fits better.

The wildebeest, on the other hand, cannot be described with such ease. They say that after God created all the other animals, he took whatever parts were left over and created the wildebeest. He's an awkward looking animal with large humped shoulders, similar to a camel's back, the thick neck of a moose, skinny legs like an antelope and a beard like a Billy goat. He has a long unkempt black fringe misplaced on his throat instead of his neck, where instead dark bands of fur look like the deep wrinkles of an elephant. He has a long horse's tail, and the rounded horns of a bull. I try desperately to come up with a name for him. Willy? Bruce? Beastie? None of them fit, just like none of his body parts fit together. His name will have to wait. For now he will just be Wildebeest.

Will they ever have a family? A herd to run with? Will anyone ever love them unconditionally? Will they have a home they can always go back to, where they will be welcomed with open arms? Or is this it? Will they always be alone? Are they afraid?

Bonty stares back at me as though we are both pondering the same big questions, and I can't help but wonder who is observing whom.

The afternoon winter sun is beginning to set. Now acquainted with our neighbors and aware of their grave proximity, our camp is even scarier than the night before. I zip my tent zippers tight and check my sleeping bag, suitcase, and every square inch for deadly snakes and flesh-eating spiders. The dim camp light will stay on for the night. Once in bed, the shadows the light cast on the walls defeat its purpose as a savior and, instead, only feeds my imagination with visions of spider webs and silhouettes of hungry lionesses.

"Good night, Melissa. Will you take another swim in the mud pit tomorrow?" Melanie begins to laugh hysterically.

I pull the sleeping bag up tight just under my ears, leaving them open to hear anything that lurks outside.

"Good night, Melanie, and don't let the lions bite," I whisper through the tent wall.

With that, Melanie goes quiet, and it's another sleepless night in Africa as my demons awaken and drag me kicking and screaming to that ugly, dark place I keep running away from.

"Mum?" My voice is soft, I hope she is asleep. Her hospital room is dark except for the faint glow of Christmas tree lights I had hung around the window. Christmas cards fill the windowsill.

"Yes," she answers, wide awake.

"Why are you still awake?"

"We were waiting for you."

"Who?"

"Me and your father."

My father had died the year before. The awkwardness is immediately broken when she speaks again, this time pleading, "When can I go home?"

"Soon. I brought you some of that chicken you like from that place around the corner."

Her whisper is faint. "Will I be home before Christmas?"

"Of course you will." I'm careful not to look at her, fearing she will see the doubt on my face. I begin to rearrange the Christmas cards.

"Don't throw away any of my Christmas cards. Let's take them home with us, I want to keep every one of them," she says proudly.

"I won't throw them out."

I roll up her bedside table and begin unpacking the take-away boxes and plastic cutlery.

"I'm scared, Melissa." Her eyes pierce my own with an unbridled intensity.

"Don't be scared, Mum. Let's eat the chicken while it's hot. Come on, I'll help you." I can't look at her. I know if I do, I will lose what little control I have left.

"Can you just lay with me, instead?"

"Of course." I push aside the bedside tray. Relieved to be out of her line of vision, I lay down beside her.

"Where are you?" she asks. Her brain has shut down all feeling on her left side.

"I'm right here beside you. Try to sleep."

Within moments she is in a deep sleep. I lay wide-awake, as I do every night, and regard the ceramic Christmas ornaments beside the cards on the windowsill. The little mice carrying sacks of presents with smiling faces and twinkling eyes are reminders of Christmases past, only the mice don't fit in this depressing hospital room with the nauseating antiseptic stench. There is no joy or excitement in this room, no matter how much I try to bring Christmas into it with the decorations, cards, and lights. I can't bring the past back, and nothing can mask the ugliness and horror that is growing with each day that passes. Reality overshadows everything.

I would do anything for the aliveness of Christmases past. The Christmases that, admittedly, I didn't always look forward to—the stress, the bickering, the family feuds—but it was all bliss compared to this. I never imagined I would spend Christmas alone watching my mother's life slip away in a hospital bed. Bargaining and begging, I offered God my limbs, my eternal service, and even my life if He would just change the present circumstances. How ignorant I was to not appreciate family before it was too late.

Outside, pristine snow falls on the North Shore Mountains surrounding the city, the air is clean and crisp, it is a perfect winter night. But inside, nothing is perfect.

"I can't live without you, Mum. Please don't die. Please don't leave me." I whisper the words into her ear and clench her hand tightly.

5

Committed

I am still awake when the wretched screech of the Hadeeda echoes through our camp at sunrise, just like it did the day before. Their presence is a welcome relief, as it signifies that night has passed.

I emerge from my tent to what is perhaps one of the most inspiring sights thus far in Africa. The sunrays reach up high from behind the towering mountain range, stretching their long golden arms towards the sky. It looks like the brilliant reflection of gold from a gigantic pot just out of sight. As the rays creep up, the colors begin to dance across the sky. Shades of yellow and gold gently waltz along the horizon, kissing the top of the soldiers' fur caps. They're joined by a vibrant, jazzy salsa of every shade of fiery red and orange, as mandarin, tangerine, and even scarlet make appearances, followed by the crescendo of pink, lavender, and purple. I have never witnessed a sunrise as stunning as this. I am grateful to capture this memory and imprint it for an eternity in my mind. It will be my sanctuary for the future dark days when Melanie is gone.

I make a run for the volunteer house to grab a quick tea, and there I find Melanie already showered, dressed, and looking very ready to leave. I can see the relief in her eyes, knowing her last night in the tent camp has passed without incident. Her bus doesn't leave until noon, but I can tell she's been ready for hours.

"Melanie, did you sleep in here last night?" I laugh.

"Yes, I did," she says, obviously exhausted. "It's not safe here, I have a terrible feeling, and I think you should come to Cape Town with me."

"I can't go to Cape Town, I came here to volunteer."

"But you have already volunteered on the elephant reserve in the townships. You have done enough. This place is dangerous."

"I'm not ready to go yet."

"And Gerrit—he is a tyrant, how will you stand being with him day after day? He is an awful, awful man."

"You're right, that will be difficult. It'll be like working for a Drill Sergeant." I begin to laugh, and snap my fingers. "That's what we'll call him from now on, the Drill Sergeant."

"Melissa, I'm not joking. Please come to Cape Town. You can go to the games and press parties, and stay at my hotel. You'll love it. What will you do here? Work, and then what? Sit in your tent alone for twelve hours a day, until an elephant or rhinoceros tramples you to death?"

"What's going on? Are you ready to start working, or what?" It's the Drill Sergeant, formerly known as Ranger Gerrit, standing in the doorway of the common area.

"She is coming to Cape Town with me," Melanie states.

"That's a great idea." It is the first time the Drill Sergeant shows any genuine emotion other than anger.

"Yes it is."

He looks over at me and asks with a mocking undertone, "Is it really true? You're leaving us this morning?"

Time stands still as I weigh the options before me. A luxury hotel, unlimited access to the World Cup, and media parties sound very alluring . . . and safe. Maybe Melanie has a point, and maybe I have seen enough of this place already. The Drill Sergeant certainly doesn't want me here—neither does that filthy, horrible elephant, Kittibon. But running to Cape Town wouldn't fulfill the reason why I came to Africa.

Melanie and the Drill Sergeant aren't the only ones in the room. An old skeleton has appeared and begins to present his case.

~~~

"You have to get a life." My oldest sister's harsh words slice through me. My siblings have come to town and have called a meeting in the restaurant across from the hospital.

"I have a life."

"No you don't. You're there every day and every night, sleeping in that awful hospital room."

"What about her? She has no choice but to be in that awful hospital room. I can't leave her alone. She's afraid."

"It's not just that, you need to get a life, in general. You have no one, just her. The rest of us have our own families. Soon, she'll be gone, then what do you have?"

I thought I still had a family. I thought her passing would bring us all closer. I thought we would support each other. Won't we?

I expect one of my other siblings will jump in and tell her to stop. Tell me that we are family and that we have each other. Family is supposed to stick together, especially in hard times. Blood is thicker than water, or something like that. But no one says anything, their faces are expressionless. The busy restaurant is filled with tables of happy families, and mine has just imploded.

"We want to put the house up for sale," she continues.

"What do you mean? She's not dead yet," I shouted, not giving a damn about the glances from neighboring tables. "What happens when she tries to go home and there is no home to go back to? What will you tell her, then?"

"She can't look after herself anymore, she can't live alone. We're going to go through the house tomorrow, get rid of some of the crap in there before a real estate agent comes to look at it."

"Crap? It's not crap. That's a family's life in that house, her life, Dad's life, the first thirty years of my life are still in that house!" Rage overtakes me. How can she be so cold?

"We won't touch your things, but we want to clean it up before we leave town."

"Leave town? You just got here yesterday, why are you leaving?"

"It's Christmas Eve tomorrow, we need to get home to our own families."

My brother avoids my eyes, and my other sister looks at me with great sadness. She knows this is wrong, but she wants to avoid conflict.

"You can't leave Mum on Christmas. I've arranged to have Christmas dinner catered in her room. She loves Christmas, and she's so happy everyone will be here this year. Don't do this to her." No longer asking, I'm begging them, which is like begging a stone to have a pulse. My mother may have lost feeling on one side of her body, but she is aware of everything around her. She doesn't think she is dying.

"The doctor isn't optimistic, so you need to face reality. She's dying." My sister's tone is as cold as ice.

"The doctor doesn't know her, he doesn't know how strong she is. She's going to get better, she just needs love and support. Miracles happen every day." Even though I plead, my words have no effect on the strangers seated around me. I'm furious. If we all pull together we can save her. She needs all of us here. She is our mother, dammit. "How can you leave her?"

"We're leaving tomorrow night," she says with an air of finality. "Let's get the bill and get out of here."

"She'll be looking for all of you, it's Christmas! What the hell will I tell her?"

The skeleton fades away until it's just Melanie and the Drill Sergeant left. It's no longer Christmas, and my siblings are gone, but I feel that same sense of defeat in the room.

"Right. I'll see you ladies at 11:30. I'll drop you at the bus stop, and you'll be on your way to the World Cup in no time." The Drill Sergeant, polite and still smiling, sounds like a different person.

"I'm not going anywhere."

"Melissa!" Melanie cries.

"What?" His smile disappears.

"I'm staying right here. I'm ready to get to work whenever you are." I'm not going to give in again.

"I will remind you again that this is not some sort of a spa getaway. Nor will this compare to what you see in those silly Hollywood movies. There is nothing glamorous or romantic about this place. This is real, and it's hard work. There's no room for complaining, whining, or crying. You will still be expected to work, even if you do complain, whine and cry." He waits a beat before continuing. "You will get dirty, cold, and tired—and even then, you will still be expected to work, to do whatever job we give you, or Mother Nature dictates."

"Okay."

But he isn't finished pontificating, "Mother Nature is unpredictable, at best and wildlife is even more unpredictable than her. My job is to keep you alive, but if you make stupid mistakes and take unnecessary chances, I will not risk my own life to save yours."

"Okay."

"Do you understand?"

"Yes."

The Drill Sergeant begrudgingly tosses me a pair of soft butter yellow leather gloves and a camouflage green baseball cap. "You're going to need these," he grunts. The smile, long since disappeared, has been replaced with a scowl.

"I'm going to need some kind of a weapon too."

"We don't carry guns at this reserve. We use our brains, and above everything else, we use our common sense—I hope you brought some of that with you." His voice trails off as he stomps out the door.

I give Melanie a long hug, and we vow to meet in Cape Town in a few weeks' time. I turn to catch up to the Drill Sergeant, who is already beeping the horn and shouting something in Afrikaans. Life is finally beginning.

6

Think Tank

A current of excitement and adrenaline pulses through my body, and I can barely contain myself for the exciting work that lay ahead on my official first day of work at the Big Five Game Reserve. Perhaps I'll be working in the cheetah breeding program, or maybe I'll get to dart a rhino. Or maybe we'll just observe the socialization behavior of giraffes, or track leopards. Or maybe the Drill Sergeant will teach me some safari survival skills now that I'm living alone in the tent camp, like how to wrestle a croc.

This is the most exciting day of my life. Unable to hold back, I jump into the seat beside the Drill Sergeant. Ack. I hadn't seen the pool of condensation in the seat. The back of my jeans are completely soaked.

With a turn of the ignition, the air is filled with the pungent smell of fuel. After a loud huuucccckkkkk, we take off on our first adventure. I'm not even going to ask what we'll do first because I want to be completely delighted and surprised when we arrive to our first mission. I'm dying with anticipation, and my cheeks hurt from the grin plastered on my face. I don't even care that I'm sitting in a cold puddle—bring it on. I will take whatever this day is going to give me. The sun is high and bright and my yellow leather gloves are flawless, just like the day ahead.

The Drill Sergeant drives only a hundred yards, stops, turns off the engine, and gets out of the truck in front of the elephant stables.

"Why are you stopping?" I ask. I'd seen enough of that wrinkly old bitch yesterday and have no desire to see her again.

"Time to shovel shit." He averts my eyes and slams the door behind him with a loud thud.

Are you kidding me? I didn't come all the way here to clean out elephant stables. Surely there must be some kind of a mistake, or this is a cruel joke. I look back at the common area, and I have sudden visions of press parties, good food, and five star hotels. Do I go, or stay here and shovel elephant dung? What if he makes me shovel shit every day? What if that's all I ever do here?

"Hurry up, woman!" the Drill Sergeant shouts.

I enter the stable and watch Kittibon closely, keeping far away so she won't be able to launch another dung bomb at my face. She turns her head and stares at me through the shadows of the pillars with one big brown eye. Even her glare makes me squeamish, but I can't let this cow see my weakness.

"What are you staring at, cow?"

"Careful, you don't want to make Kittbon angry."

I glare back at the Drill Sergeant. "And she doesn't want to make *me* angry. I'm the one who has to clean her house, so she should be nice to me."

The Drill Sergeant leaves to open the back door of the stables to let the ellies out, so we can move in and start our momentous task.

Kittibon, still watching me, curls her trunk around a long branch then holds it high above her head, as though she's cocking it like a gun.

"Don't you dare . . ."

SWACK! She hurls the branch and wallops me alongside the head with great force.

"Ouch!" I scream, while running for cover behind a stack of Lucerne.

"What's going on in there?" the Drill Sergeant shouts from the back door.

"That damn elephant threw a branch at my head."

"I told you not to make Kittibon angry."

"Don't lecture me, help me!" I scream.

"Hold on, I'm putting them out. She's more interested in her mud bath than trampling you."

Once the elephants are safely out of the stable, the Drill Sergeant hits me with his own bomb. He tells me that today we will not only remove the soiled sawdust, but we will remove *all* the sawdust. Then the floor needs to be scrubbed and disinfected with bleach. While the floor is drying, the feeding trays need to be scoured out and refilled, and finally, the pillars will need to be hand-sanded where the ellies have damaged them. This is not the important conservation work I thought I had signed up for. This is bullshit.

The Drill Sergeant hands me a shovel that looks as prehistoric as the elephants and weighs as much as one. "You can use this."

I try to muster up some of the energy and excitement I had only moments before. "Where do we put all this crap?"

"I'll pull Harrison around, and you can pile everything in the back. When the bed gets full, come and get me and we'll go unload it."

"Come and get you? Aren't you going to help me?" I try to hide my horror at having to do this shitty job alone.

"I have some calls to make, I'll be back just now." *Back just now?* In my world, *just now* means, well, now. I can only imagine what it means here.

He disappears faster than I can open my mouth in protest. I don't even know where to begin. I've never mucked out an elephant stable before. It can hardly compare to kneeling beside a kitty litter box using a tiny plastic shovel to remove finger-like droppings.

Standing in the middle of this elephant litter box, because that's all it is, everything, and I mean everything, is of elephant proportions: the box itself is huge, the rusty metal shovel I'm using weighs about thirty pounds, and is missing half the handle. But the worst part is the dung itself. Each piece of elephant dung is the size and weight of a bowling ball. And elephants aren't light eaters. They eat and dispose of a few hundred pounds of waste a day, so there are enough bowling balls in here for a national competition. The sawdust is soaked in urine, making it even heavier and smellier than the dung.

After an hour of shoveling ellie dung, the layers I wore for warmth are long gone, my jeans are still damp, and my back feels like it's broken. I've made almost no progress. I can't lift more than one dung ball at a time, and the weight of the urine-soaked sawdust limits each load to half a shovel full.

Outside, I can hear the Drill Sergeant on his radio, speaking in Afrikaans and laughing. He's probably talking to the other rangers and laughing at me, telling them that he'll break my spirit and have me running for the bus before noon, or at least wishing I had.

The smell of his cigarette smoke mixed with the smell of urine is nauseating. I move mountains of heavy, stinky, sloppy sawdust, and lift load after load of heavy balls of dung, exhausting my strength to the point where my arms and legs are now shaking.

I pause and look around the stable; it still looks untouched, but to give up now is not an option because my failure would be a success for the Drill Sergeant. I will not give him that. I will not give him anything. The work is grueling and the most difficult physical job I have ever done. It allows the mind time to wander, since it doesn't require any cerebral activity to shovel crap.

Soon my mind shifts into survival mode, distracting my body from the pain and fatigue, by trying desperately to mend loose ends from the past.

As soon as the elevator doors open I can hear my mother's cries in the hospital corridor. I sprint to her room, where I see her sobbing uncontrollably to the nurse. "I'm sorry, I'm so sorry, please don't make me leave. I said I'm sorry, it was an accident."

The nurse's face is set in a stern glare. There is nothing nurturing or compassionate about her. I don't like her. She treats my mum with indifference, as though she's an inconvenience. Her thick ankles patrol these halls like a sergeant, shouting orders and demeaning anyone who dares show weakness. Deep-set frown lines litter her face from years of unhappiness. "Stop crying," she barks. "We have to move you to change the bed."

"What happened?" I ask, running towards my mother.

"It was an accident, and now they want me to leave, to go to some horrible place where people die. It was an accident, just an accident, I'm sorry."

The nurse is abrupt. "She soiled her bed, and we need to move her so we can change the sheets,"

"It's okay, Mum, no one is taking you anywhere. They just want to change the sheets."

"Actually we're moving her to a hospice in the morning," the nurse states.

I am aghast. "You want to move my mother to a hospice on Christmas morning?"

"Yes, we have some papers for you to sign at the desk."

"Why can't I just go home?" my mum cries. "I just want to go home, please take me home, please."

I look directly at the nurse. "Can I please see you outside?"

She follows me outside, and I close the door behind her. "Why is my mum being moved to a hospice? She's not dying. If you send her to a hospice, she'll give up, and she'll die for sure. No one ever comes out of there alive."

"There's nothing we can do for her here."

"And what? Now she's an inconvenience to you? Well, I won't let you move her, and what you can do for her is make her feel comfortable and not ashamed when she has an accident. The woman is paralyzed from the neck down, goddammit!"

I push past the nurse and into the room where the other nurses have moved my mum into a semi-horizontal wheelchair. I wheel her into the lobby where a man is playing Christmas carols on the piano. Hot apple cider and Christmas-shaped sugar cookies have been set out. I move her close to the piano. She loves Christmas carols and the music quickly relaxes her.

After some familiar songs, the pianist speaks to me. "I wrote the next song for my own mother, it's a very special song. I hope you will like it." He begins to sing in a somber tune, the lyrics describe a boy whose mother dies on Christmas.

I can't listen, it seems everywhere I turn, everyone has lost faith, and everyone believes my mum is going to die. I push my mother past him and out onto the deck into the brisk evening air to catch my breath.

"Do you believe in miracles, Mum?"

"Of course. We are all miracles, walking, breathing, loving miracles. Don't you?"

"Yes. I believe in miracles, too."

After several minutes we return to the warmth of her room.

The stable door creaks behind me, where the Drill Sergeant stands and watches me work. "How you making out in here? Almost done, I see. Good."

"No thanks to you." *Lazy, no good, chauvinistic jerk Neanderthal.*

It has taken me nearly five hours to clean the stable. He didn't lift a finger other than to hand me a shovel. He is a jerk of elephant proportions, and I don't want to work with him. He has no personality to speak of, and and manners are as foreign to him as his accent is to me.

My new gloves are no longer butter yellow, they are black, wet, and have lost their shape. What's worse is that they won't even stay on my hands. I had to resort to picking up balls of dung by hand and lobbing them into the back of Harrison in an effort to save my back from the weight of the shovel. Underneath, my hands that these gloves were meant to protect are badly calloused and blistered. The inside of my thumbs are raw where several layers of skin have been rubbed off, and the mere touch of the gloves on my skin is excruciating. My shoes, socks, and clothes are soaked in sweat and elephant piss, and our workday isn't even half over yet.

"I'll go dump this, and when I come back we need to load eight bails of Lucerne into the back of the truck," the Drill Sergeant says.

"What's the Lucerne for?" I thought it was just for these filthy elephants.

"Drought has dried up most of their food source, so we subsidize the diets of the big animals. After that, we'll go and feed the cats."

"Cats?"

"Lions."

"What do the lions eat?"

"Meat."

Hopefully they only like lean meat and not the fatty, blonde city variety.

The Drill Sergeant returns a few minutes later and says he'll meet me in the store room *just now* to load the Lucerne, but it's no surprise that he is nowhere to be found again.

I eagerly begin to carry a bail of Lucerne out to the truck. Each bail weighs sixty pounds, but feels twice its weight. The heavy-duty plastic string binding each bail cuts through my gloves, rendering them useless.

Unable to take full steps, I shuffle outside dragging the bail. Once outside, I try to toss it into the truck, but it's hopeless. It bounces off the tailgate, back onto me, and knocks me onto my butt. My new Big Five Volunteer t-shirt I'm proudly wearing is covered in this sticky grass. It's actually weaved itself right into the fabric of my shirt, itching and scratching my skin underneath. The day can't possibly get any worse.

I look around, hoping that the Drill Sergeant hasn't just seen what I've done and, thankfully, he's out of sight—likely having another smoke while I do the heavy work. I try once more to toss it up, swinging it backwards first to gain momentum, and then lob it up with all my strength, but again it bounces off the side of the truck.

Mumbling obscenities, I return to the storeroom and shuffle out with another bail. Before I even reach the truck, I trip on what appears to be a hardened piece of elephant dung. I don't have time to put my hands out in front of me because these stupid, useless gloves are stuck in this stupid bail that has now fallen apart because I fell onto it. The Drill Sergeant arrives and graces me with a disapproving look. He picks up two bails at a time and lobs them into the truck with ease. He's not even wearing gloves, and there isn't a shred of grass stuck to his shirt. I don't think I could possibly dislike a person any more than I dislike him right now.

"Take lunch. I'll pick you up in thirty minutes," he barks.

This has been the crappiest Monday morning of all time.

7

Circle of Life

Lunch is a chocolate bar and hot tea while I bake my shoes and gloves in the oven at 400 degrees, trying to dry them out.

The Drill Sergeant arrives as I'm getting back into my shoes. "Get in the back of the truck."

"Why?"

"Because you're going to distribute the Lucerne."

It sounds like a luxurious task after shoveling ellie shit all morning and shredding my hands. And what a bonus, I don't have to sit beside him. I climb into the back of Harrison, making a seat out of a bail. As we exit the gate, Kittibon decides it would be great sport to block the road. The Drill Sergeant honks the horn, but she doesn't move.

He shouts out the window. "Hold on!"

I have a death grip on the rim of the bed as he veers off the road and through a gully to get around her. She reaches her trunk into the back of the truck to steal some Lucerne, but she's not fast enough.

"Ha ha! Nice try, cow!"

The Drill Sergeant hollers back at me. "Don't harass her. Elephants never forget. She'll get revenge if you piss her off. Kitty always does."

Not if I can help it.

On the edge of camp stands the lonely Bonty, looking out over the fence into the open reserve, watching and waiting, as usual.

"Helllllooooooo, Bonty!" I yell. "You are not alone," I whisper under my breath as we pass him.

He seems to look at me as though he knows exactly what I said.

After several minutes of driving over rocky makeshift roads, the Drill Sergeant pulls off the road, slowing Harrison to a stop. "Get a bail ready," he shouts.

I look around, there's nothing but scrub brush. Nevertheless, I remove the string and jump down from the truck.

Within seconds, out of the brush, making his way towards us is a giant African buffalo. His horns are massive, and he's coming quickly towards the truck. I start throwing grass towards him, and soon one after another, several buffalo are trotting out from the brush, all heading straight towards us. I pull apart the grass as fast as I can to disperse it before they arrive. They're thundering toward us at full speed. I stand tall, awaiting our first meeting.

"Get in the truck!" the Drill Sergeant barks, through puffs of his cigarette.

"I don't want to get in the truck. I want to watch them eat from here." I've had just about enough of his orders for today.

"That bull will pulverize you into the ground with his head in about twenty seconds," he says with indifference, not even a hint of concern in his voice. Instead, his tone implies that it would be an inconvenience for him to have to clean up my pulverized remains.

I get up in the truck just as they arrive. They eat like wild pigs, snorting and grunting, tossing grass everywhere. I imagine this is what the Drill Sergeant looks like when he eats.

"Buffalo kill more people every year than all of the Big Five combined. Never underestimate the rage of a buffalo."

We leave them to eat, and carry on with our patrol. Soon, we encounter the mother rhinoceros and her baby. The baby is named Habiby — Arabic for "darling."

"Why has her horn been cut down?"

"She has been fighting with the male so much since the baby was born that it cracked. To save it, we had to cut it down to half size."

"Why is she fighting with the male?"

"Typical female behavior, really. She won't let him near her since she gave birth a year ago, and if he tries to come around, she beats the crap out of him."

"That is not typical female behavior."

"Mother Nature reflects human behavior. Anyway, it's most likely the root cause for the male's aggression, and why he's undergoing hormone therapy — lack of love and affection."

"Are the hormones working?"

He nods uneasily. "For his aggression, but not so much for his manhood. He still has random acts of aggression, but he's getting soft and sensitive. The female is getting more vicious now that she sees he's getting soft — again, typical female behavior."

"Have you ever considered hormone therapy for yourself?" I laugh.

"No. Have you?" He fires back without missing a beat. If only he had the same gusto when it came to cleaning the elephant stable.

The rest of the patrol is done in silence until we reach the maintenance building.

"A quick stop in here, then we'll feed the lions."

He goes inside, leaving me outside for several minutes. I get out to stretch my aching legs. I walk around the back of the shack, out of sight of the rangers inside. I can't let anyone see that I am suffering from the grueling work — especially the Drill Sergeant.

As soon as I turn the corner, I hit a wall of the most pungent stench ever imaginable. It smells like what can best be described as rotting death. My nose immediately goes on strike and refuses to inhale. I open my mouth to breathe and instantly gag, as I can now taste whatever this is. I pull my bandana over my face, but this proves to be no obstacle for the reek. It is now in my eyes, making them water uncontrollably. I gag with more force this time, bringing up bits of the chocolate bar I ate for lunch. This stink is fierce, and it won't back down. My senses are refusing to give in to it, and each and every orifice is fighting for survival.

I run in circles trying to escape this sensory invasion. I can't go back to the front of the maintenance shack because I'd rather die than let the Drill Sergeant and the other rangers see me gagging. I make a dash for what appears to be a makeshift tarp-covered shed, thinking I'll hide in there until I can collect myself and stop gagging.

I sprint into the shed, but am stopped dead in my tracks as I run smack into the source of the revolting odor. There's a large hook hanging from heavy wire cable that stretches from one side of the ceiling to the other. Suspended from the hook is a cow — or what is left of a cow. It doesn't have any legs and there is raw flesh everywhere. I turn to run out, but the floor is slippery, and I almost lose my balance on the blood-soaked concrete.

I walk with quick, long steps directly back to the truck. A moment later, the Drill Sergeant comes out. "You could have come in."

If he was polite enough to ask me in the first place, then there wouldn't be bloodstains on my shoes, a stench from hell stuck in my sensory membranes, and the vision of a mutilated carcass forever emblazoned in my memory.

He drives Harrison to the rear of the building and loads the carcass into the back. I stare straight ahead. "What's the matter?" he asks.

"Nothing. What happened to that cow?"

"She couldn't stand up after she gave birth. When that happens the farmers call us. We shoot the cow and bring it back here for cat food."

"That's horrible."

"It's the circle of life, it's natural, and it's normal. Everything dies, and it's what it leaves behind that matters. That cow is leaving behind her remains to give life to another animal."

"It's still horrible."

"What's horrible about it? Death is an inevitable part of life. The sooner you accept it, the easier life will be."

There's nothing black or white about life and death. Nor is there anything final about death. Sometimes death takes on a life of its own.

The cab goes quiet again as we leave the maintenance area.

I am no stranger to Death. In fact, Death haunts me every day. I wish I could accept him, but he's an ugly beast who lacks civility. The last time I saw him, he stole everything that was sacred to me.

"Merry Christmas, Mum."

"What is this?" She smiles like a child as she looks at the box in my hand.

"Your Christmas present."

I bend over her and fasten the silver chain around her neck, adjusting the crystal heart to sit in the center.

"There we go. It looks beautiful. You can wear this on New Year's Eve."

"I love it, thank you. Your Christmas present is still in my bedroom closet, go get it and bring it back here."

"I'll get it later."

"But I made it for you. I want you to see it now."

"I'll go to the house tomorrow, it's Christmas, let's just watch some Christmas movies"

"Where is everybody?" she asks, confused.

I don't have the heart to tell her that everybody left town, with the exception of one sister who wanted to be here, but is at home with the flu.

The Drill Sergeant abruptly interrupts my thoughts again, "Are you all right, Melissa? Does the cow really bother you that much? I've never seen anyone cry over a dead cow before."

"I'm not crying. I'm allergic to the Lucerne."

8

Feeding The Cats

The first gate opens and Harrison crawls into the holding pen to wait for the gate to close behind us before the next one will open. They call this a *security measure*. I don't see the security in this if we were being chased by lions and had to get out of the camp in a hurry. We would make it to the gate only to die waiting for it to open. There isn't even an emergency door close by, just in case one had to take to the ground and make a run for it.

This time, there is no Melanie at the window seat, a barrier between the lions and me. This time, the door will not even close, and it flapped around the entire way here on the pothole-infested road. Each bounce threatened to take it off its hinges, retiring it for good. This time, I'm terrified to go into the lion camp because I know what is waiting on the other side.

"There they are," the Drill Sergeant says.

My throat tightens as my heart jumps into it. Are they going to chase us again? What are we in for now? How does this work, exactly? I've never fed a lion before.

Two fearless lionesses begin sprinting head-on towards the truck in a game of chicken. They're closing in fast. Each one of their running strides is nearly the length of the truck. No one is backing away—even old Harrison is picking up speed.

Huuuuuuuuccccccckkkkkkk.

The lead lioness is only a few feet in front of us. She will be on top of us in less than a second. She is sprinting so fast, her face is pulled back, and her eyes are wide with ferocity. I squeeze my eyes shut and brace for the impact. The Drill Sergeant veers to the left, and I slide hard into the gearshift between the front seats. There are no working seatbelts inside Harrison.

"Hold on," the Drill Sergeant says, in an oddly calm voice. His green eyes are ablaze.

"To what?" I scream. There's nothing for me to hold on to, not even a door handle. My whitened knuckles grip the edge of the seat, nearly tearing through it. Despite my death grip, I'm being tossed around like a rag doll, and my head smashes against the tin ceiling with every rock we run over.

This is insane. "I can't hold on anymore!"

"Are you ready to go to Cape Town, yet?" he yells back.

Bastard.

I wedge my damp shoes deeper into the holes of the rusty floor for more stability. The Drill Sergeant takes a sharp left around a tree, and my door flies all the way open. Momentarily suspended in the air, I see myself rolling out the open door into the path of the lions.

"I don't have a seat belt, or even a damn door! Stop driving like a mad man. I'm going to be tossed out!" He's trying to kill me.

"It's easier to do this with only ONE person in the truck," he shouts back.

Harrison speeds up a steep hill, the lionesses still right behind us. Huuuccckkkk, huk, huk, it sounds like Harrison is gasping for air, and may run out of steam.

I scream above what sounds like Harrison's dying gasps. "What *is* that? Is this truck dying?"

"Don't worry, Harrison's a champ, he won't let us down!"

I can't tell if he's trying to convince me or himself.

We come over the crest with an abrupt jolt. It's even steeper on the other side. It will be a miracle if Harrison stays in one piece after being subjected to this thrashing.

Harrison nose dives over the edge and takes off down the hill. He is at his maximum speed, and the pedal is on the floor. The speedometer reads forty miles per hour. Not good, considering lions can run at speeds of fifty miles per hour. Harrison remains vigilant as he careens over large rocks, and doesn't even hesitate as he takes out walls of scrub brush. He's horking and choking, but carries on with unrelenting determination.

The lionesses are still in hot pursuit, and not far behind them, the male has also joined the chase. They're not even panting, it looks like an easy jog for them. I, on the other hand, can barely catch my breath from holding on for dear life inside this tin suicide box.

The Drill Sergeant leans forward over the steering wheel, searching the ground to avoid major obstacles.

"I have to stop," he finally says.

"What!" I scream. "Why?"

"I have to open the back, let the carcass out."

"You're going to get out of the truck? Are you crazy?" Of course he's crazy. He's driving like a madman and has me hanging onto a shred of metal that is the single barrier between life and playing a harp with the angels.

He's going to be eaten alive if he gets out. They're right behind us! What is he thinking? He can't die out here. If he dies, what will happen to me? I'm going to be the one who gets stuck in the holding pattern of those stupid gates with a lion clawing me out through the busted window.

Harrison bottoms out briefly in a ravine, but then speeds up to the other side. Hallelujah. I breathe a sigh of relief, but it's quickly snuffed out by my growing anxiety that the Drill Sergeant is going to get out of the truck. Can I even remember how to drive a stick shift?

Harrison slides to a grinding halt. The Drill Sergeant leaps from behind the wheel and sprints to the back of the truck. I can't watch, I don't want to look back. The last time I did, those lions couldn't have been more than a hundred yards behind us. I hear the clunk of the back open, and a fraction of a second later, the Drill Sergeant is back in the driver's seat.

With a loud *hhhhhhuuuuuuuuukkkkkkk*, the transmission is jammed into reverse. We are now speeding down the hill backwards in another game of chicken with the lions. I jam my feet harder into the rusty holes, the sharp metal pinches them, but it's nowhere near as painful as rolling out my door into an awaiting lion. The Drill Sergeant slams on the brakes, and I slam into the dashboard. The carcass torpedoes out the back with brute force, gaining height and speed, it hits the ground with a large thud. The lions stop to inspect the drop.

The Drill Sergeant turns off the engine and tells me to sit quietly and not move. I can't move or speak even if I want to. I'm frozen.

After what feels like several minutes, my heart resumes beating, and I carefully remove my camera from its case. I press the ON button, and out of the silence emerges a *bing bing bing* from my camera. The Drill Sergeant glares at me. Damn you, Canon for not having the foresight to silence this feature for situations like this, when a harmless melody could stir up the aggression of a lion, finalizing this life or death situation.

I expect the lions to pounce on the carcass and feast, but they don't. All three of them are watching us, instead. The male sniffs the back of the truck and leans forward. He opens his jaws and a long, fat pink tongue slowly emerges. It licks a disgusting glob of sticky, gooey blood off Harrison's back and returns to his mouth. It arouses him. He won't be satisfied with an already dead prey, he wants . . . more.

I stare out the back window in a frozen state of raw terror — fear has long since vacated. My eyes meet his, and I can't pull away from his stare. *Don't make eye contact, you idiot.* It's hopeless, I can't look away even though my life may depend on it.

His canine teeth hang over his lower jaw like daggers, long, sharp, and pointed. The wind blows through his shaggy black and brown mane, whipping it around his face and into his eyes, but he still doesn't flinch. A golden inferno burns within eyes that are lined in charcoal black. Focusing their intensity, they scorch right through me, rendering me powerless under his spell.

He is six-hundred pounds of solid, ripped muscle. Each one of his front legs is thicker than my body. But his real strength lies in his jaws with a bite force of 1,000 psi.

"He likes you," the Drill Sergeant whispers.

"I wish he would like you, instead," I whisper back.

The lions have no experience in the wild. Why aren't they going for the carcass? They must think that Harrison is an animal, and they have captured him. Now they are calculating their attack. These lions have no fear of humans and never before has it been more evident than now. Why aren't they going for the beef? Is it because they can smell the chicken sitting in this truck, and it's more appetizing?

One of the lionesses skulks to my side of the truck and lies down. She can't be more than five feet away from me. She's staring at my reflection in the side mirror as I look back at her, watching for any sign of movement. I curse the open window and useless door that she could easily pull me out of.

The words on the side mirror read: "Objects are closer than they appear." If she were any closer she would be in my lap. The rush of adrenalin leaves my body trembling. I can feel my temples pulsing, as my brain screams for more oxygen in order to remain on high alert. My heart is wedged in my throat. This must be the Drill Sergeant's plan to get rid of me now that there are no witnesses — feed me to the lions!

The lioness slowly stands up and takes one step forward towards the mirror. One more step, and she will be here. She is not afraid.

A faint whisper emerges from my dry lips. "Gerrit…?"

With a loud *hhhhhuuuuuuuuukkk*, we lunge forward. The huntress follows, sprinting now to keep up with us, still on my side of the truck. The Drill Sergeant accelerates and Harrison obeys, taking us up the hill at full speed. About halfway up, the lioness stops. Thank God.

"Was she pursuing us?" I ask.

"Seemed like it, didn't it?" The Drill Sergeant lets a grin slide across his mouth.

I search his face for some kind of a sign, a hint of fear, perhaps, but find nothing there except aloofness.

We watch as the lions begin to devour the carcass. They peel off the hide and it snaps back in resistance like a rubber band. The flesh comes off in long strips and ribs explode under the effortless pressure of the male's jaws. Soon, the carcass is unrecognizable as a cow, and the circle of life is complete.

The day is drawing to a close, and as we make our way to the tent camp, I feel a new uneasiness. My stomach starts to churn as I wonder how in the world I am ever going to sleep tonight, now that I've met my new neighbors, and now that I am completely alone.

9

Terror at the Ritz

"You're late."

Standing over me is an attractive young man with gorgeous green eyes. He's speaking in a thick, foreign accent, and it's difficult to make out his exact words, but I think he's just said something sultry like, "You're great."

I love it when my dreams are enriched with details like this. Don't wake up, don't wake up . . . I just know this is going to be an amazing dream. It's so real. It's as though I can reach out and touch his strong arms that are crossed in front of his even stronger chest, or follow the line of his rigid clenched jaw with my hand. I wonder why my imagination has made him look so authoritative and cold in this dream. Come on, imagination, soften him up a bit, or better yet, make him look like Dwayne Johnson.

He's sexy in his khaki shirt and jeans, that have just the right amount of snugness. His skin is tanned and golden. Maybe this dream is set in the tropics. I love the tropics. Maybe he'll give me a hollowed out coconut with a paper umbrella in it. Then maybe he'll offer to lather me up with sunscreen while telling me how amazing I am, curves and all. He loves a woman whose dress size isn't of preschool age. Oh yes, this is going to be a lovely dream indeed.

"What the hell are you doing in here, woman?" he suddenly barks.

Crap, this isn't a dream. I'm awakening to the ongoing nightmare I'm living. It's the sadist Drill Sergeant hovering over me, the man who tried to feed me to lions yesterday. I take back everything I just said about him being attractive, and all those other ridiculous thoughts I was having in my near comatose state from physical exhaustion. He's not attractive, he's repulsive. And dammit, he's caught me sleeping in the common area.

"There was something in the tent camp again, and this time it was something big and deadly."

"It was probably just the rain."

"The rain? It rained?"

"Yes, it rained. First real rain we've had in a hundred years."

"Is it still raining?" If it's raining maybe I won't have to work today.

"No, but a huge storm is forecast in the next few days, so get up," he grumbles. "We've got real work to do today."

Barely able to lift my aching bones from the floor, I head out to my tent to get ready for the second day in hell, working for the devil.

Before I can make my escape, he begins to laugh hysterically. "I knew you wouldn't be able to sleep in your tent. I just knew it, ha ha ha!"

It was true. I'd spent the night in the common area. I had every intention of sleeping in my tent last night, I really did. But circumstances beyond my control took over and forced me to spend the night inside.

It had been a long first day on the reserve, and the Drill Sergeant's plan to force me to leave was nearly a success. Cleaning the elephant stables was backbreaking work, and enlightened me to dozens of muscles I never knew I had. I'd returned to my camp and gulped down a simple dinner to allow longer time in a hot shower, where I could warm my bones and relieve my throbbing muscles. I didn't waste any more time than necessary, since I wanted to be in my tent before dark.

There's no heater in my tent, but once all the flaps are closed, the heavy canvas turns it into an insulated cocoon that's quite warm when one considers the outside temperature of 40 degrees Fahrenheit. The canvas is heavy enough that it blocks out all sunlight.

The problem was that afternoon brought with it a light dusting of snow on the mountains. The wind picked up the chill of the frost and delivered it into the valley, dipping the mercury below freezing by the time I retired to my lonely tent.

Once there, I layered my clothing for the night with two pairs of heavy socks, long johns with my jeans on over top of them, three shirts, and a jacket. I went through my nightly ritual of checking in between all the sheets and blankets—just in case a snake or spider had snuck into my cocoon, also seeking refuge from the cold. Thankfully, my search was fruitless, and I tucked myself into bed, pulled the covers up high, just under my ears, and gently slid my arms out so as to not disrupt the positioning of the blankets. It was 6:30 pm.

I thought about Melanie, who is probably enjoying a steak dinner at her fancy hotel in Cape Town or watching television in the comfort of her posh room. Maybe she's walking around downtown in the crowds of fans who came from around the globe to see the World Cup. I tried desperately to think of anything other than my neighbors, and that's when I hear it.

Raaaarrrrr. My heart stopped. A lion. *Raarrrrrr.* It sounded like it was right outside my tent. Could it be? It had to be.

It must be the male. I could see his desire to devour me earlier. He must have followed my scent of fear back to the tent camp.

Raaaaarrrrrrrrr. Holy shit. Maybe it's the lioness; she knew I was no match for her. She mocked me at Harrison's window, and could have taken me then, but she, instead, chose to wait. She's waited until dark, until I'm stranded in my tiny tent camp alone. She terrorized and taunted me from the other side of the canvas. In truth, she doesn't need to kill me because I'll die from fear itself. Then she can drag me back to the lion camp and share my flesh with her pride.

Grrrrrrrrr. What the hell was that? It's a different growl, not a lion—I don't know what, but it definitely came from right outside my tent. Oh God, the walls are shaking! I wasn't imagining this, I could see them. Wait . . . was it just the wind? Couldn't be, could it?

Snorrrrrrt. What the hell was that? Something horrendous. Something deadly. Snnnnooooorrrrtttttttt. Oh God. That wasn't the brownie-eating porcupine. It was much fiercer. Whatever it was, it probably just ate the damn porcupine!

I had to call 9-1-1, only in Africa it's not as simple as 9-1-1. Now what was it? I saw it on the back of a police car once, I should have written it down. It was something like: in case of an emergency, dial 8649283764521839800. Who the hell will remember that?

I quietly reached over and picked up my cell phone. I hadn't even turned it on since arriving here, and didn't know if it would work. I wracked my brain about whom to call. Perhaps the operator could send help?

I held my hand over the speaker hard, so it wouldn't make any noise turning it on. *Please God, please God, give me a cellular signal.*

It felt like an eternity for my phone to turn on; finally, the screen lit up, and I searched for a signal. *Come on. Don't do this to me. All I need is one bar, just one bar to make a call.* No bars. *Please, God!* No bars, not even one. I try to dial anyway; maybe it just isn't showing the signals. I pushed zero and hit Send, but it was just dead space. My chest tightened. I could't breathe. I didn't even have a weapon. How could the Drill Sergeant not have left me some kind of a weapon to defend myself? He doesn't want me to be able to defend myself, that's why. He wants me to perish out here. Then he won't have to bother with me.

I heard footsteps now, but I couldn't tell if they were the footsteps of a man or an animal; they sounded heavy, and they were moving slowly around my tent, pacing, pacing, pacing. *Oh God, I can't believe this. I should have gone to Cape Town. I am an idiot, a first rate, certifiable idiot.*

Maybe it was the Drill Sergeant out there. Maybe he was trying to scare me. *It must be him. It has to be.* I tried to whisper hello, but nothing came out. On second thought, maybe it was safer not to speak; what if wasn't him, and I alerted the killer that I was in here? *What if it's a murderer, a strange man, a vagrant who has found his way into my tent camp? There are fifty murders a day in South Africa — of course I'm going to be one of them! Maybe the word got out that there's a woman sleeping alone in a tent camp . . . without a weapon . . . or a cell phone signal.*

My eyes darted from one wall to the other. I knew that any second now one of these tent walls would crash in by the force of an animal pouncing on it. Either that, or I'd see a knife slicing open the canvas wall. Wait, this is Africa, it wouldn't be a knife; it'd be a machete, a long, silver machete. No, wait, I had to keep my eyes on the zipper; if it was a man, he'd open the zipper, not slice open the side of the tent with his machete — that only happens in horror movies. Or does it? Oh God, I didn't know where he'd come in!

The walls flapped ferociously in the freezing wind.

I couldn't move. I was frozen. Even my breath escaped me. I couldn't take it anymore. I surrendered. If they had any shred of decency, they'd kill me quickly. Holding my breath I waited for my inevitable death.

At least I'd die in Africa. At least I'd die taking a chance, doing something worthwhile (is shoveling ellie dung really worthwhile?). I wondered if they'd bury me here, or fly me back home. Maybe there wouldn't even be anything left of my body, or maybe they'd never find it because the beast would drag my remains far away and bury them. Would I feel it when he bit me? Predators usually go for the throat, so if he got my jugular, it would all be over quickly, but it'd be messy. Would I see my own blood spraying out of my throat, oh God, this was going to be gory.

But wait. What if it was a man? What would he do to me? It would probably be a slower kill. I'd fight him. I'd go for his eyes. Yes, I would poke his eyes out with, with, with what? My chapstick? It didn't matter. I'd poke him in the eyes with something and disable him. After that, I'd kick him where it counts, and then run and scream bloody murder until someone came to my rescue.

If it was a man, I'd have a better chance of surviving. What if there were two men? No, I didn't think there were two men out there. There could only be one, two made no sense. Two was irrational, wasn't it? Or was it? I had to think logically. I had to keep my wits about me.

I listened hard, but heard nothing. It was quiet outside. I slowly peeled back my blankets, careful not to make any noise at all. If the Drill Sergeant was out there, I would have him crucified for this.

Slap! The tent wall caved in and immediately blew out again. Even the wind was getting more aggressive. Anxiety was killing me. I couldn't take it any longer; I had to get out of this tent. I didn't even have a flashlight.

Just do it, just get up, open the zippers and make a run for the common area.

I can't move.

You can do it.

No, I can't.

Yes, you can.

Outside was complete blackness, which meant I couldn't even see my attacker before he got me. How would I know what killed me? But if I stayed in here, heart failure would kill me for sure. I had to make a run for it.

I moved slowly toward the door, not making a sound. Why did there have to be two sets of zippers? It was painfully slow opening the inner zipper, one tooth at a time, stealth-like, without a noise. If I was quiet enough, I could surprise the predator and buy myself an extra second or two.

I moved to the outside set of zippers. *Breathe, I can do this.* With each tooth that opened, I felt the bitter cold wind on my hands that were trembling with fear.

I was terrified, and I'd never been so scared and angry with myself for signing up for something as crazy as this. But there was no time to cry or beat myself up, I had to get out of here alive.

Please, please, please don't let me die out here, not alone, not now.
Focus. Once that flap opened, I was going to run for my life to the common area four-hundred feet away. The side zippers opened, and the final one was the center zipper.

I was still on my knees and getting up into a crouched position so I could push off from my feet, like sprinters do, to get an extra strong start. 1...2....3. I yanked open the zipper and took off, running in stocking feet. I could see the faint lights of the common area in the distance—my target, my goal. Tears were streaming from my eyes as I ran with lightning speed, like a gazelle, zigzagging back and forth, to throw off my chaser. All my focus was on the common area, I didn't even waste time to breathe. *Don't look back. Don't turn around. Focus on what is in front of you. Focus on the shelter. You can do this. It's life or death.*

I fumbled with the door handle and ran in. I couldn't believe it. I made it. I stood at the door; one of those farmhouse-style doors where you can close the bottom and keep the top half open, and hid around the corner. But no predator slammed into the door. No one was hacking at the door with a machete. There was nobody there; nobody but the wind and the distant echo of the lions next door.

It was freezing in the common area, and there were no blankets in here. In my hasty escape, I neglected to bring a blanket. I piled up some cushions into a makeshift bed and laid down. I was still terrified, but there was something comforting about being surrounded by concrete walls. I was exhausted, utterly and completely mentally and physically drained. The Drill Sergeant had worked me harder in one day than I had worked in my entire life, and it was only just beginning.

I had survived terror at home, and now I'd faced death here. And this was only my first night alone in the tent camp . . .

10

Chopping Down Barriers

"What are we doing today?"

"We're going to the dump," the Drill Sergeant grunts. Not very exciting, but anything is better than shoveling shit. "Then we're going to cut branches for the ellies."

"Oh." *I hope I don't end up a campfire story like the guy who nearly castrated himself.*

It's the first time Harrison isn't waiting outside. This time it's a different white pick-up truck.

"Where's Harrison?"

"In the shop. Flat tire. This is Cruiser."

Cruiser is in much better shape than Harrison—there are no holes in the floor, and he doesn't have a chronic transmission cough. Instead, his engine purrs. However, Cruiser is far from perfect, and he has his share of ailments, too. The door handles and rearview mirror are barely held on by tiny metal wires, rendering them nearly useless. There are no luxuries, such as a radio or air conditioning, and the windows are permanently closed in this truck, instead of open like in Harrison.

Cruiser has come with a partner in tow, a rickety, tired-looking and severely handicapped trailer stuffed with garbage bags. It has old bent-up chicken wire for walls, and a back gate whose fastenings are more bits of the same heavily worn wire. Without the hundreds of fragments of wire, this truck and trailer would be in pieces.

After an hour of driving in silence, save for the clackety-clack of the trailer, we arrive at the dump on the outskirts of a small farming town. The dump is shaped like a crescent moon, with mountains of garbage as high as a three-story building. The stink in the air is nearly as disgusting as the carcass from the other day. At the entrance, six men are sitting on crates turned upside-down playing cards. Their faces are expressionless. Each one is clad in heavily stained and torn dark-blue coveralls. They are uninterested in our arrival. One of them nods us in. I'm not sure what their purpose is, since we don't have to pay, and they didn't even look at our load. Maybe it's just a way for them to pass time in this sleepy town.

The Drill Sergeant takes several minutes to undo the mess of twist ties holding the trailer gate on. He is careful not to drop any of the sacred wire, and re-attaches each piece for later use.

As we begin to unload the garbage, a man appears, out of nowhere. He's not one of the gatekeepers, there are still six men there. Fidgeting his hands, he approaches the trailer, avoiding eye contact. Something is off. The mountains of garbage begin to move all around us. Big white eyes appear in the shadows—lots of them.

"Gerrit," I whisper.

He ignores me. He's too focused on the tiny scraps of wire and doesn't realize we are about to be swarmed by a garbage gang.

"Gerrit, I think we're in danger."

"Why?" he mumbles, without looking up.

"We're surrounded."

The man is already beside Cruiser.

"Hello," I say to him. My God, I'm about to be a statistic, and I can see the headlines now:

American Murdered at Garbage Dump in South Africa!
Remains tossed in with the other garbage. Aloof and stupid ranger never even noticed volunteer was murdered!

The man doesn't answer, he doesn't even look at me. Instead, he's fixated on our garbage. He stands at the end of the trailer, eyeballing the shiny black bags, but doesn't touch them. Then, with a nod from the Drill Sergeant, he snatches a bag and scurries away, hunched over it with arms tightly grasped around it. Just as fast as he leaves, another man comes forth out of the shadows. He doesn't speak either. The Drill Sergeant nods and he takes a bag, too. The first man is in front of Cruiser, crouches over his bag, carefully pulling apart its contents.

"What are they doing?"

"Some are pig farmers. They collect garbage to feed their livestock. But most are looking for food to feed their families."

"Are you serious?"

"Yes. Haven't you seen this before?"

I shake my head. "Never."

I've seen people fish for bottles in dumpsters before, but I had no idea an entire subsystem existed at the dump.

"It's very competitive. They're all looking for the lekker load, something ayoba."

"Lekker? Ayoba?" Are these some type of African vegetables?

"Yeah, ayoba."

The Drill Sergeant frequently speaks in Afrikaans dialect, forgetting I don't understand it. Or more likely he just doesn't care that I don't understand.

"That's why they wait here all day. They want to have first pick."

More and more people appear. The Drill Sergeant lights a smoke and walks away from the trailer. I follow him and watch as the trailer is emptied for us. The garbage bags are flying off the trailer in every direction.

A virtual litter market has opened in front of the truck, and there are people everywhere. Two men argue over the contents of a bag and it rips, scattering potato scraps all over the ground. Several men drop to the ground, stuffing this hot commodity into their pockets and down their shirts. Another man barters melon scraps for rib bones. One man stuffs used tissue paper into his pockets — nothing goes to waste.

It's an incredible scene; an entire economy exists in the dump with multiple transactions taking place, the only currency being garbage.

The men at the gate are still engrossed in their card game, not paying any attention to the events taking place behind them. The Drill Sergeant pays no attention, either. Instead, he meticulously ties each little tiny wire back together and rebuilds the walls and gate of the truck, taking him nearly twenty minutes. I don't understand how he has great patience for monotonous tasks, but no patience for eager volunteers from the city.

We leave the dump that's still buzzing with activity. The trailer shudders, threatening to rip apart when Cruiser passes over some old railroad tracks. A well-aged and rusty rimmed sign bearing the name Tinia is posted beside the tracks — some of the letters are missing, but its purpose is served.

Small, picturesque, quaint houses begin to speckle the landscape. They're constructed of wood, and most of them are painted bright white with black-shingled rooftops. They're from the colonial era, many a few hundred years old. Even this tiny sampling of civilization is a sharp contrast to the game reserve.

The lone road leads us to the town square where there are a number of small specialty shops — a butcher, a produce store, a shoemaker — and the bright-pink liquor store or *Doepke* in Afrikaans. The Doepke is tempting, it would make dealing with the Drill Sergeant a little more palpable, but his propensity to work me past exhaustion defeats the enjoyment that would come from a bottle of Merlot.

In the center of town is a huge wooden church. The white paint that covers its timbers is gleaming in the afternoon sun, like a welcoming beacon that beckons weary followers to its doors; we speed past.

As Cruiser and his accompanying trailer rattle through town, pedestrians turn to look at us, and as they do, I wave at them.

"Stop waving at people," the Drill Sergeant barks.

"Why?"

"They'll think we're weird, and I know most of these people."

"You know most of these people?" It's hard to imagine the Drill Sergeant actually knowing anyone. Surely he doesn't socialize with people, does he?

"I grew up here."

"You did? In this little town?" Interesting, he has a past.

"My family's been farming here for a few hundred years."

"Really? Where is your family's farm? Can we go see it?"

"No."

He says it so firmly, that I mutter a quiet 'okay.'

The air grows thick in the cab with a long, awkward silence. The Drill Sergeant is unaffected by the silence, but it's getting to me. We always work and drive in silence. At night, I'm alone, in silence. My only neighbors are Bonty and the wildebeest, and no matter how much I talk, they answer in silence. I need some human interaction here.

"Well, farming sounds interesting. Tell me about it."

"There's not much to tell. If your farm is doing well they take it away from you."

"What? Who takes your farm away?"

"*The government*, that's who. It's no good to have a farm anymore."

"Well surely you can just say no—no one can force you to leave."

"It happens all the time."

"How can anyone make you leave?"

"They show up at your door and give you twenty-four hours to pack up your shit and leave. If you're still there when they come back, they will murder you and your family on the spot."

"My God. I can't imagine . . ."

"You don't want to imagine it."

"Did that happen to your family's farm?"

The Drill Sergeant goes quiet again. The deeper I dig, the darker he gets, the more questions I ask, and the more I need to keep digging.

"You must be afraid."

"I'm not afraid."

"Well maybe you're not afraid, but it must be difficult . . ."

He shuts me down with a dismissive huff. Is this why he's so jaded? It would make a little more sense, but either way he's not going to let me in to find out.

I follow his cue of silence and focus instead on the little town.

We continue down the long, straight road and abruptly stop at the first stop sign I've seen in a few weeks. It's quickly apparent that the intersection is some type of boundary line.

The neighborhood across the street is exactly opposite to the one we just drove through. The beautiful, quaint homes have disappeared and have been replaced by clapboard shacks, the kind Melanie and I saw in the townships during our first week in South Africa. The dwellings are built of mismatched pieces of plywood, sheet metal, even flattened cardboard boxes are used as siding.

Occasionally, there is a tiny house, perfectly rectangular, in between these dwellings. These houses are Government Issue, but built so poorly that they usually fall apart within a couple of years. Each one is about ten feet wide by fifteen feet long, but what's even more surprising is that, on average, ten people live in one of these ill-constructed boxes. My little tent seems like a luxury when compared to this.

Even though the houses are tattered and run-down, their gardens are filled with bright hand-painted pots, blooming flowers, and handmade artwork that adorn the spaces, taking the focus off the fatigued structures they surround.

Apartheid officially ended in South Africa in 1994 when the first democratic election was held, but here, in this small rural town, the reminders of separateness still exist, as they do in many parts of this country. As we pass people, I continue to wave. No, I don't know what it means to live here, and I don't pretend to. But what I do know is that everyone deserves to be seen.

In the city, it's easy to look past strangers, in fact, it's weird to wave or smile. However, here in the boroughs of Africa, I can't stop myself. I don't know why it makes a difference here, but it does. There's something about Africa that invokes compassion, humanity, and gratitude for not having to find my next meal in a garbage dump.

'We're almost there," the Drill Sergeant says, breaking the silence.

Africa is teaching me to live in the moment, even if it is out of necessity, rather than enlightenment.

"Why do we have to cut branches for the ellies? Doesn't that go against nature?"

"There aren't enough trees on the reserve because they've eaten them all."

"But doesn't that take away from their natural instincts if they don't have to find their own food?"

"Yes, but we scatter the branches in the elephant camp so they still have to find them. It's not exactly the same, but it's the best we can do on our small reserve."

Makes sense, I guess.

At the end of town, Cruiser turns into a long dusty alley and stops. The alley is lined with small trees and dotted with tall King Proteas, the national flower of South Africa. Each King

Protea has one massive flower measuring almost a foot across. The center is rimmed with pointed petals resembling the sun, and possesses the same energizing and illuminating effect. They look like fashion models swaying down the runway at six feet tall, dressed in the most elaborate shades of pink, purple, magenta, yellow, and orange. Their colors appear to come from the same swatch as the morning sky; bold and beautiful. There are hundreds of different varieties of Protea, and at least five varieties are right here in this abandoned alley. I can't help but admire their beauty.

Thud. A rusty machete lands near my feet.

"You can use that silly old one." The Drill Sergeant turns quickly and heads into the trees.

I don't even know how to hold a machete. Granted, I don't have a scrotum, but I could just as easily chop one of my legs off with this thing.

"Hey!" I try to stop my commander-in-chief before he disappears, "I've never used one of these before."

"Just pretend the branch is your ex-boyfriend and whack it. I'm sure you can do that, can't you?"

That's no help. Pretending the branch is the Drill Sergeant would be far more effective, but I'm not ready to risk an amputation.

I watch him for a few minutes to see his technique. He shimmies up the tree with the machete in his mouth. With one arm around a branch he spreads his legs, positioning his feet far apart on opposing branches. He raises his other arm above his head. Swack! The machete cuts through the branch like butter. Swack. Swack. Swack. One after another, giant branches fall to the ground.

I'll start with something smaller. A tree not much higher than my waist is the first target. I widen my stance and square off with the little tree.

The Drill Sergeant's voice trails from the tree. "That machete can slice hairs."

Focus. I can do this. I will not amputate my leg. I will chop down this tree. I slash the tiny branch with all my strength, but nothing happens. Dammit. Whack. A tiny piece of bark ricochets just near my eye, but other than that there is no damage.

The Drill Sergeant is in his own world, not paying any attention to me—no encouragement, no training. Nothing. I try again, this time, with short bursts of chops, one right after the other, fast and furious. This produces nothing more than tiny notches in the bark. Even the damn tree is mocking me. Chop chop chop chop chop chop. Out of breath and dripping with sweat, I examine the tree. Nothing. It's got to be the machete.

"Heyyyy!"

The Drill Sergeant ignores me.

"I said, hey!" I throw my arms up in the air for effect.

"What?"

"This machete sucks. It's useless. Can I try yours?"

"Sure." He smirks as he tosses the machete onto the ground.

I try chopping an even smaller tree this time. Still nothing happens. Goddammit, there must be some type of technique to this. Maybe if I slice on an angle? Nope. What about this angle? Nada. Straight on? What the hell? From the bottom? Shit. Shit. Shit. I give up and throw the machete as far as I can before slumping to the ground. I hate machetes. I hate trees. I hate the Drill Sergeant. I hate this job. I hate everything about this place. I can't sleep in my tent. I can't go one day without being assaulted by an elephant. I can't do anything the rangers can do. I can't even use a goddamned machete. I'm useless. That's why he makes me shovel shit day after day. I should have gone to Cape Town. My bottom lip begins to tremble uncontrollably. Hot tears burn my eyes. Stupid fool.

"Why don't you collect the branches instead?" The Drill Sergeant barks. *And stop crying.*

Even he has noticed how completely useless I am at this job. And worse, he saw my breakdown. Well I'm not done yet. Someone has to collect the branches.

We work in silence, other than the repetitive *ting, ting, ting* of his machete. I lay the branches evenly in the trailer, lining them up perfectly. There's nothing to my job, and the Drill Sergeant knows it. Trying to make piling branches in a crappy old trailer look like thought provoking, important work is fruitless.

To make the most efficient use of space in the trailer, I jump up and down on the branches. They finally break under my weight. Didn't need a damn machete after all.

"Make sure you lay them flat," he orders.

"I know what I'm doing, thank you very much."

"I guess there's a first for everything."

"Excuse me?" My blood pressure starts to rise and I'm about ready to tell him what he can do with these branches.

"By the way, head office wants to know if you want to do a great white shark dive with the shark conservation group. They need to book it soon if you're going to do it."

Do I look like I'm insane? "No thanks."

"Why not? South Africa has the best white shark diving in the world."

He really is from a different species if he thinks I would even consider something so ridiculous. "Not a chance. I'm petrified of sharks. I'm not even going anywhere near the water, thank you very much."

"That's too bad."

"Why do you care if I go shark diving?"

"Because I was going to visit a witch doctor."

"For what, a personality adjustment?" All the witch doctors in the world couldn't fix him.

"No, I was going to ask the doctor to put a spell on the great white sharks just to make sure you get eaten alive."

"Very funny."

He has the potential to carry on a conversation after all. Now is a good time to start chipping away at that wall.

"What are you afraid of, Gerrit?"

"I am not afraid of anything, Melissa." His voice is stern and his eyes meet mine for the first time.

"You must be afraid of something. Everyone's afraid of something, like me and sharks."

"Nothing." He holds my eyes for what feels like an eternity. "I am afraid of nothing." I search for something in his eyes, anything. I find nothing.

At last, he relaxes and begins to chop away at the branches again. "Anyway, you can still get on the morning boat charter. I think you should go."

"I'm not going shark diving. Not now. Not ever."

"That's too bad. I was hoping that by this time tomorrow, I'd be phoning your family to let them know you were eaten by a shark," he says, laughing.

"Well maybe by this time tomorrow, I'll be explaining the awful machete 'accident' to your family!"

He doesn't miss a beat, "That's impossible because by this time tomorrow, I'll be speaking at your eulogy."

"By this time tomorrow, I'll be dancing on your grave," I shout, dancing on the pile of branches in the trailer.

"By this time tomorrow, I'll be spitting on your grave!" He spits on the ground.

"By this time tomorrow I will be p..." My foot gets lodged deep in between the branches, thrusting me flat onto my back with force. I try to pull my foot out, but it's stuck within my perfectly piled branches. By this time I'm laughing so hard, I've got no strength left to pull it out.

"In Africa, karma is instant," the Drill Sergeant chants.

Surrendering to this moment of karmic justice bestowed upon me, I sink deeper into the branches.

"Don't get too comfortable in there, you've still got elephant stables to clean today," barks the Drill Sergeant.

Crap.

11

Revenge of an Elephant

The Drill Sergeant says elephants never forget. I don't believe him. I think this local folklore is just as fictional as those "important calls" he needs to take when he leaves me alone to clean out the elephant stables.

Kittibon continues to mock me every morning by slapping me in the face with trunks full of sawdust. I thought I outsmarted her by wearing a bandana for protection—but she was smarter when the sawdust was replaced by branches whipped at my head. I couldn't let an elephant beat me, so I upped my ante as well. I've been leaving a layer of dung-encrusted shavings in her feeding tray, just below the surface to give her a taste of her own medicine. Two can play her game, but only one can master it, and master I have become. I may not be able to do a lot of the jobs around here, but I can outsmart a stupid elephant. I am convinced I've won the battle with Kittibon and proven a point to her: No four-ton prehistoric grouch is going to intimidate me.

Today the Drill Sergeant says we will be doing ground maintenance in the elephant camp. I had never considered that we would have to work among the elephants when I had tainted Kittibon's feeding tray.

"I daresay we must exercise extreme caution today. The ellies are territorial and get very aggressive when anyone's in their camp," the Drill Sergeant says.

It's as if he can read my mind.

"And remember, I did warn you that elephants never forget when you continued to harass Kitty."

Perhaps I *could* be intimidated by a four-ton prehistoric grouch, after all. What's the worst that can happen? She charges the truck and we drive away. Right? She can't be any faster than the lions.

We climb inside Harrison and cautiously head into the elephant camp. I search the horizon. Where is she? If she even looks at me sideways, we are outta here. We're on ellie turf and there are no concrete barriers to protect us in here. No sign of the elephants. Hopefully, they're on the other side of the camp taking a mud bath. I don't really care where they are as long as it's nowhere near me.

At one point this was an old farm, and our orders are to remove all the old telephone poles from the camp. They're heavy and awkward to carry, even as a team. This is going to be another painful and boring morning with the Drill Sergeant.

It is not until we are in the midst of dragging the fourth pole when the Drill Sergeant stops dead in his tracks. He is staring at something behind me. Suddenly, I see what he sees, a thundering cloud of wrinkly grey skin coming towards us like a twister. Paralyzed, all I can do is watch. Where did they come from? How do such massive creatures run so fast?

Kittibon and Selati are running with trunks raised like rifles pointed at us, the targets of their charge. Holy shit. Boom. We drop the pole onto the ground below us, which has now started to tremble under the weight of the elephant offensive.

They're coming so fast, there is no time, this can't be real. I shriek at the Drill Sergeant. "What do we do?"

His command is simple. "Hide beside the truck!"

The ellies arrive and stop just short of Harrison. Their size makes him look like a toy truck. Kittibon stretches her trunk over Harrison and inhales deeply just above my head. I don't move. I don't even breathe.

She pulls back her trunk just as she gives her head a violent shake, ears flapping and slapping the sides of her head. For the record, there are three warning signs elephants give before attacking: 1) head shake, 2) lots of noise, and 3) mock charge.

She's just given the first warning sign. We have to get out of here now. There is no way to fight an elephant, and these elephants mean business. I look to the Drill Sergeant for an escape plan, but he thinks he can scare them away.

"Get out of here!" he screams as he leans across the hood of Harrison.

The ellies retort with long trumpet blasts and push towards the front of the truck; warning sign number two has occurred. The Drill Sergeant picks up a stick and throws it at Selati. Thump. It hits him in the ear and falls to the ground beside him.

The elephants go still. Maybe this scare tactic worked.

Selati lowers his head. It worked; he's hanging his head in defeat—or is he? The finger-like protrusions of his trunk begin to delicately move across the ground. It moves over several branches and rocks, but he doesn't pick any of them up. I don't recognize this sign of elephant etiquette. But then, he pauses at the very stick the Drill Sergeant just threw at him. He curls the end of his trunk around the stick and raises it high above his head.

"Look out!" the Drill Sergeant shouts, "Elephants never miss!"

We sprint to the back of the truck, ducking down and using our arms as cover. Selati flings the stick, barely missing the Drill Sergeant's head.

The Drill Sergeant grabs a handful of stones as we both jump up into the bed of the truck. He gives me some, and together we barrage them with stones, trying to hold our position while keeping the enemy at bay, *rat, tat, tat, tat, tat.* Each stone we throw gets thrown right back at us with twice the force; all hopes of triumph are quickly slipping away.

"We have to get out of here. It's a bloody mutiny!" I scream.

"Get in the truck!" he orders, his voice shaking slightly for the first time.

He covers me with a steady storm of rock-fire, while I sprint to the cab and dive in, narrowly escaping stray pebble fire. Kittibon has seen me. She quickly springs to my side of the truck, surprising me with her agility. Her trunk comes towards my window, which is stuck in the open position, of course. Just as her trunk enters I slide over to the driver's side, only inches out of her reach. She inhales deeply; it is the familiar sound that's usually followed by a tantrum. She withdraws her trunk from the window, moves to the front of the cab, and stops. She turns her head, revealing a glaring eye. It's a standoff, the moment when two enemies come eye to eye just before they try to kill each other.

Selati is at the back of the truck snatching the poles out that we just spent an hour getting in there. The Drill Sergeant tries to hold them in, but he's no challenge for Selati.

I look back at Kittibon just as she hurls a large rock at me. It hits the windshield right in front of me, cracking the glass. The bitch has broken Harrison's face.

She moves to the driver's window and, again, encroaches with her long trunk, reaching closer and closer. Oh God, soon she will have me. I slide as far over to the passenger side as I can, but her trunk is nearly on my throat now. She's inhaling my fear, relishing the scent of panic. *Fight the fear; don't let her sense your fear. Stand up and fight, you coward!*

She is a terrorist, torturing me with all the possibilities of how she could kill me right now. I'm not going to sit here! With an abrupt push, I open my door and fall out into the wet straw. Immediately pulling myself up, I scramble into the back of the truck.

"Get back in the truck and floor it while I fend them off!" the Drill Sergeant bellows. I haven't heard this tone from him since the crocodile incident on my first day.

The Drill Sergeant launches rock grenades at the elephants. With trumpets blasting, trunks firing, and the Drill Sergeant shouting, I jump back into the cab. Through the side mirror, I catch a glimpse of Kittibon's trunk moving toward the open window again. I turn the key while jamming it into first, and the ever-faithful Harrison charges forward.

"Go, go, go!" screams the Drill Sergeant from the back of the truck. I push in the clutch, shift into second, and throttle the gas. I dare not look back. I try to find the gate far ahead while trying to find some semblance of a road while swerving around potholes the size of craters.

There are loud smashing noises coming from the back of the truck, and I catch a glimpse of a telephone pole bouncing out of the bed, that one shortly followed by another one. I search the mirrors for the Drill Sergeant and see that, miraculously, he has managed to stay on board. The ellies are charging after the truck—warning sign number three. As the poles catapult from the back, the ellies stop to inspect them, after all, the poles belong to them. This allows us time to escape.

By the time we reach the gate, there are no poles left in the back of the truck, just an angry Drill Sergeant. I stop the truck once we are safely through the other side. The Drill Sergeant jumps out and motions me to get out of the driver's seat. I do not speak or look at his eyes. The familiar veins in his forehead are bulging and his face is the darkest shade of purple I've seen to date.

Through clenched teeth he utters, "I told you, elephants never forget."

With that, we call it a morning.

12

Deciphering the Local Dialect

The Drill Sergeant has accused me of not following orders, being disrespectful, and has even gone as far as calling me a renegade, saying that my actions would be considered treason in some countries—this all over a small elephant incident that can hardly be blamed on me. How does he expect me to follow his orders, when half the time I can't understand what he says, and those words I do understand have a completely different meaning than what I'm used to? I could argue that he is just prejudiced against me for not understanding his jibber jabber, but he probably wouldn't understand my exposition spoken in plain and simple English.

Instead, I have been forced to study his local dialect because an all out war is on the horizon—a clash of cultures caused by misunderstanding, miscommunication, and ignorance . . . on his part, of course.

Interpreting his expressions hasn't been easy, since there's no such thing as a direct translation. The vocabulary is wrapped in cultural nuances and then further entangled in customs and traditions, which one needs to be immersed in to fully comprehend. I am nowhere near this point, but I am, at the very least, able to make some sense of the basic demotic vernacular that I am exposed to daily. During this exploration, it has become apparent that words that have a specific meaning in other parts of the world mean the exact opposite here. This knowledge has come at the high cost of frustration, and even, at times, humiliation on my part.

South Africa is a diverse and culturally rich country and for this reason, they call it the rainbow country. It has eleven official languages: Afrikaans, English, Ndebele, Northern Sotho, Sotho, Swazi, Tswana, Tsonga, Venda, Xhosa and Zulu. In this farming area, I've mainly been exposed to Afrikaans, a rudimentary form of the Dutch language, born here in the 17th Century with the influx of Dutch immigrants.

I have compiled a small sampling of the most common phrases and sounds I have been exposed to at the game reserve. There are many more that I have not listed, as I am still trying to figure them out myself — a task not easy to undertake.

- **Ag Shame** - It doesn't mean too bad, or that's a shame, as it does in the rest of the world, instead it means "sweet" or "adorable."
- **Howzit?** - How are you? Spoken very quickly, with no delay in between "how" and "zit."
- **100%** - Common expression meaning that's excellent or utter perfection.
- **Ayoba** - You are ayoba or that's ayoba. This means "totally awesome." It is the highest compliment to be called ayoba. So far, I have not received this compliment.
- **Braai** - Literal translation in Afrikaans is, "roasted meat," but in practical terms it means barbecue. Braais are very popular in South Africa and are a rich part of this country's culture. Ostrich and Kudo make for excellent grilling meats, I've heard, but wouldn't know from practical experience.
- **Lekker** - This means "the best." For example: the *braai* last night was *lekker*. The current volunteer is *lekker* — even if her immediate supervisor doesn't realize it yet.
- **Hectic** - Brutal, terrible. It doesn't mean crazy busy, as it does back home. Once, I told the Drill Sergeant that it looked like it was going to be a hectic day with all the work we had to do. He didn't understand what I meant

by that, and he told me to have a positive outlook and not denounce things before they started.

- **I dare say** - The Drill Sergeant uses this at the beginning of nearly every sentence, regardless of the content. For example, "I dare say you are one of the most hectic volunteers I've ever seen." I know this is used in many other places, but I've never seen it used as much as it is here, and in such loose context.

- **I promise you** - Also very common, this can be translated as, "I am serious," or, "I mean it." But when the Drill Sergeant says it, there is no sincerity in it whatsoever. He may as well be saying, "I don't give a damn about you," or, "I curse you."

- **I must say** – If the Drill Sergeant doesn't start a sentence with one of the above, it is always started with this one. At first, I was awaiting some grand revelation to follow this statement, but it was usually followed by something like, "I must say, the bomas need a deep cleaning tomorrow morning."

- **Buy a Donkey** - The only Afrikaans word the Drill Sergeant has taken the time to teach me. It is really spelled *baie danke*. It means thank you very much, and I dare say I haven't had much practice in having to use these words with him.

- **Where's that funny old . . . .** - While on our morning patrols, the Drill Sergeant always says, "Where's that funny old lion?" Or "Where's that funny old buffalo?"

- **Where's that silly old . . . .** - When looking for lost tools, the mileage book (that is supposed to be filled out daily, but hasn't been once since I've been here), or any material item, the Drill Sergeant uses this expression. For example, "Where's that silly old machete?" or, "Where's that silly old shovel?" I can only hope he doesn't use this expression when he's referring to me, such as, "Where's that silly old volunteer from the city?" But I wouldn't be the least bit surprised if he does.

- **Don't make me strip my mood on you** – This is an expression that I've heard the Drill Sergeant utter at me more than a few times. I think it means don't make me lose my temper with you, but I can't be completely sure.
- **Playing with a lion's testicles** – There is nothing perverted about this expression. It literally means to take chances because to try and play with a lion's testicles would be very risky, indeed.
- **Just now** - This expression has, by far, caused me the most grief since I have been here. The term "now" means the exact opposite as it does back home. There is nothing *now* about it. It literally means "later," and I have no idea why they put the word" 'just" in front of it. I think it must only be to add further confusion to this sloppy expression.

As if the language barrier didn't present enough confusion, I have to deal with the sounds as well. Yes, sounds. God help me.

- **Long whistle** - Many times while I was reciting a story, the Drill Sergeant would suddenly break into a long, drawn-out whistle. It doesn't come at the climax, nor does the whistle come at the end of the story as feedback. The whistle can be heard at any random time, and most of the time it comes when you least expect it.

  Bottom line, if you hear a long whistle when you're talking, just continue talking. I think it may be a way of acknowledging you're being heard, sort of like a head nod in other countries.
- *Hhucck* - This is a similar sound to what Harrison makes, but it's short and fast. It usually appears at the beginning of a sentence, but sometimes appears midway through a sentence, as a way to separate thoughts, like a verbal

comma. This may be the equivalent of "Uh," or "Um," in English.

The Drill Sergeant finds me just as difficult to understand as I do him. Large blocks of our conversation are filled with "What?" or "Pardon me?" or the inevitable, "Uh huh," and, "Oh, really?" as I try to figure out what he has just said. He says he can't understand my "American." It is obvious he doesn't understand me, which is made evident by his vigorous head nods at inappropriate times, or his silence when I deliver a punch line to a joke—anyone else would be roaring with laughter.

The learning curve continues.

13
The Wake of the Storm

The brilliant colors of the African sunrise are nonexistent this morning. There are no fiery shades of red, orange, or magenta illuminating the valley. Instead, the sky has been painted, using a palette of the darkest shades: midnight-blue, purple, and the occasional bolt of silver, all set against a background of the most melancholy, yet electrifying shade of grey. This dark, ominous energy is even more formidable than the sun's display of fiery shades. It feels like something evil is upon us.

The mountains are veiled in dark grey cloaks, hiding from the presence that has overtaken this valley, and even the Hadeeda are noticeably quieter this morning.

"Did the storm keep you awake all night?" the Drill Sergeant asks.

"Storm?"

"Didn't you hear the storm?"

I hadn't heard a thing. Nothing. In fact, I have a confession to make. There is a slumbering scandal that has been unfolding here at the reserve, and it is this, I didn't sleep in my tent last night. All right, I haven't slept in my tent once since Melanie left. Instead, I spend my evenings in the common area, like a stowaway, seeking asylum from the darkness and dread of that awful tent.

What's worse is that I'm relishing in this scandalous act, even going to bed early and sleeping like a log. I was even awakened by my own snoring last night, and I don't mind saying that it's glorious—every single moment of inactivity. Just to sleep within concrete—to feel its cold, strong walls around me—gives me intense satisfaction and unspeakable pleasure with the knowing that I am somewhat safe.

My justification for this cowardly act is a strong one. I work hard all day under the iron rule of the Drill Sergeant, doing demanding physical labor, and I can't afford to spend sleepless nights in my tent, staring at the ceiling and imagining all the ways I'm going to die at the mercy of a wild animal or a lunatic drifter in the middle of Africa. Who can blame me for wanting to avoid certain death out there?

Every day I clean the elephant stable . . . alone. Then the Drill Sergeant fills my afternoons with more tedious physical labor or, if he's in a good mood, he'll have me do species data collection. Thus, I need my rest to remain alert and capable.

There's no harm in me absconding to the common area night after night. After all, no one knows I sleep there. The Drill Sergeant caught me the first time, but I have never slipped up again.

My buddies, the Hadeeda, wake me up faithfully every morning, allowing me enough time to sneak back to my tent before the Drill Sergeant arrives. I wait until I hear him pull up outside, and only then do I emerge from my tent—with my shoulders back and chest puffed out—stretching as though I've just awakened. I've got the act down so well, he doesn't know any different. And besides, I don't see him sleeping in a tent. He's got a small house on the other side of the reserve. So that's my confession, and I ain't sorry for it.

Our first stop, as always is the elephant stable. My face is covered with a bandana and a hat protects my head. Not a morning passes that Kitty doesn't launch bombs or branches at me. Needless to say, I've stopped lacing her feed.

This morning, the elephants are pacing and anxious to get out. Maybe the old cow will spare me an assault for once. The Drill Sergeant goes outside to open the back doors for them as I prepare to load bails of Lucerne into the truck for our morning patrol.

Kittibon stops pacing when she sees me and goes straight to her water tub. She begins feeling around the bottom of it with her trunk but it's empty. She turns her head and stares at me with a big brown eye through the pillars. She almost looks sweet as she bats her long curled eyelashes. What? No branches? No dung?

"Are you ready to call a truce now Kitty?"

She doesn't budge.

"You started this whole thing. First it was shit in my face. Then when I covered my face, you hit me in the head with branches. Why? What did I do to you? I clean your house, I cut branches for you. Well, okay, I *pile* branches for you. I'll admit that what I did to your tray was wrong, but you almost killed us the other day. That's not right."

Her stare deepens.

"All right, I'll get you some water but you better be nice to me from now on."

I lob the hose into the tub from a reasonably safe distance and turn on the tap. Kittibon begins filling her trunk. The Drill Sergeant opens the rear doors and Selati bursts outside. Kittibon continues to drink. The water level quickly descends, her trunk inhales faster than the hose can fill the tub. Poor thing must be dying of thirst.

SSSSHHHHHHHHHHHHHHHHHHHOOOOOOOUUUUUUP PPPPP.

"ACK! You *wicked elephant!*"

"What the hell is going on now?" the Drill Sergeant yells, while running inside.

"That cow just soaked me. She tricked me. She pretended she was thirsty, and then she sprayed me!"

My hat and bandana were useless armor under the powerful force of an elephant's water-filled trunk. Kittibon, the reigning cow, saunters out the back door.

The Drill Sergeant smirks. "Elephants are smarter than people, some more than others, I see."

"She's not smarter than I am, she's just vindictive!" I screamed, wiping off my face.

"I warned you not to piss off the ellies. You're lucky she didn't kill you when she had the chance."

"I'll get her for this."

"Enough fooling around. We have to go evaluate the damage from the storm."

The storm has transformed the valley into an unrecognizable state. Entire roads have disappeared, washed away by rivers of rain. Trees have been snapped in half and scattered by the wind. The grounds that use to be dry, cracked, and dusty are now drowning in thick mud.

Mother Nature's fit of rage is devastating. "It looks like a different place, I can't believe it."

"It's a tragedy." The Drill Sergeant's voice is heavy with concern. This exhibition of emotion from him is almost as eerie as the dark sky.

"Isn't rain good after so many years of drought?"

"A little rain, yes, but not this, this is gonna screw up everything. The entire ecosystem is in shock."

The Drill Sergeant has a hard look on his face. Is there a faint whisper of sadness under his steely exterior? He inhales deeply on his cigarette, too distracted by deep thought to exhale. Instead, the smoke curls out of his lips and hangs in the thick, moist air. The end of his cigarette reaches his fingers, he doesn't even notice when it begins to burn them. "There is a pregnant giraffe here, I want to find her and make sure she survived."

"Okay, I'll look for giraffes."

"And look for the baby rhinoceros, too."

"Do you think it's that bad?" I didn't realize rain could have such a profound effect on wildlife.

"I don't know. Sometimes it takes a few days to realize the effect on the animals. The cold and damp can get into their lungs and cause a fatal respiratory infection. The young and older ones are most susceptible."

Even some of the main roads are nearly decimated from the storm. Harrison has difficulty gaining traction.

"We're going to have to rebuild these roads," the Drill Sergeant says, grinding the gears while urging Harrison uphill.

"Do you have heavy duty equipment to do that?"

"No. We'll repair them the South African way . . . by hand."

I knew it. Nothing is done the easy way here, and everything is done by hand, machete, or with a rusty old tractor from the turn of the century. Harrison takes a sharp turn and slides through the mud to a long stop just in front of a harem of grazing Cape zebras. The zebras are native to this area and flourish here. Mating has been strong and their numbers continue to grow. A zebra's stripes are unique to him, like a human's fingerprint, it's how we identify them in the field.

"Good morning, Zebras! Have you seen the giraffes?" I call out, trying to lighten the situation, but no one answers, not even a head nod. Instead, they answer me with a chorus of anal acoustics. The lower digestive system of a zebra is extremely vocal due to their hind-gut fermentation process that allows them to digest larger amounts of food in a shorter period of time. It is a highly efficient system, but the byproduct is copious amounts of gas.

"Get out of the way!" the Drill Sergeant shouts. "Damn zebras. All they do is run and fart, run and fart."

We leave the tooters behind and continue on in search of the giraffe. In the distance, a small head with little ears and horns appears just above the tree line.

"Look there!" The Drill Sergeant doesn't try to contain his excitement.

The female giraffe hides behind a clump of sagebrush when she hears the truck approach. She doesn't realize she is not hidden by a bush half her size.

"She looks fine, yep, just fine, she is." There is noticeable relief in the Drill Sergeant's eyes.

I untie a bail of Lucerne, and throw a clump on top of the sagebrush to make it easier for her to reach. The expectant mother pulls apart small pieces, chewing each one several times. Giraffes are nature's gentle giants, timid and shy, despite their towering size and strength.

Suddenly, the thundering of hooves hammering the ground cause the giraffes to bolt, leaving their breakfast behind. 'We're about to be ambushed by a herd of hungry wild buffalo.

Hhuuuuuuucccckk. Harrison's spinning wheels splatter mud onto the faces of the buffalo already gorging on the giraffe's breakfast. They're uninterested and couldn't care less as they chew in a near-hypnotic state.

I hold on tight to the bails of Lucerne while Harrison fishtails down the muddy trail. My new role is to search the horizon for anything that seems out of the ordinary, to scope out any situations that need expert attention, but all I see is mud. Until…"Stop, stop!"

There, right on the side of the road is a rare site, something that one would be lucky to see even from a distance, but up close it's miraculous. It's too good to be true. Lying down, with her legs folded up underneath of her, is a magnificent red hartebeest. A cousin of the antelope family, she is bigger and more powerful than her smaller relatives. Her horns are longer than Bonty's and curve backwards at the top. Her beauty steals my breath.

There are only two hartebeests on the reserve, one male and one female. They have been together as a pair for as long as the Drill Sergeant can remember.

Harrison rolls closer to her but she doesn't move. This isn't natural. Wild animals run away. She isn't budging. My insides turn empty and my heart tightens. She's dying. Or maybe she's just cold. She'll be fine now that the storm has passed. Any minute now she's going to stand up and run away. Please, stand up. Run away. Get out of here! Go! She doesn't move. She only looks at us, undaunted by our presence. In her dark eyes is an unprecedented wisdom and strength; there is no fear present in those eyes. Her head is held high and her shoulders are broad, a noble creature even when in a vulnerable position.

Has she been attacked? Why won't she move? Her dark red fur is soaked right through and a pool of mud has started to take form around her shape. It's obvious that she has been here for a while.

Something catches my eye, and there on the side of the hill, not far above her, is her partner. He takes a few steps towards her, but quickly retreats. He repeats this several times. Our presence is causing him stress.

Looking at the Drill Sergeant confirms that something is wrong; his face is heavy. His eyes are full of sadness. The pit in my stomach is deepening. Hope is quickly fading. Searching his face for some sign of hope, I find none. He senses me looking at him and shakes it off, replacing it with his usual stone cold aloofness. But it's too late, I've seen his human side.

He picks up his radio and says something in Afrikaans.

"Will she be okay?" *Please say she will.*

"Hard to say, these animals don't do well in the cold."

"Can we do something to help her?"

"No, it's out of our hands. This is Mother Nature's domain," he says coldly.

"Are you sure? She looks like she's suffering." Her coat is soaked, and she is too weak to stand. If a cheetah finds her she's finished. We can't just leave her here like this.

"Sometimes Mother Nature is harsh. That's her prerogative as the world's most powerful woman."

The further away we drive from the hartebeest, the closer the male gets to her. Like a faithful committed partner, he waits by her side, guarding her, protecting her, and comforting her, but knowing that he is helpless in saving her.

He looks hard at me, and I at him, and I feel what he feels. I know his anxiety, his sadness and the way his insides are twisting into painful knots, sickening him. I know his rage, his trepidation, and his overwhelming fear to be alone. Above everything else, I know his feelings of helplessness. That goddamn feeling of vulnerability when you realize how powerless you are, and how unfair and cruel life can be, and how, no matter how hard we try to convince ourselves otherwise, we are not in control.

Sitting on a stack of Lucerne in the back of a beat-up truck in the middle of Africa, those feelings are still able to invade me, just as they did on that Christmas day in the hospital room. And it makes no difference that I'm here, on the other side of the world because death's power keeps me trapped in that ugly little room. And I hate everything about it. I hate the antiseptic stench. I hate the beige walls and cheap beige laminate flooring. I hate the privacy curtain that doesn't keep anything private. I hate the nurse with thick ankles. And I hate the stupid little ceramic mice with their stupid stockings full of gifts that litter the windowsill. But I especially hate the demon that is killing my mother and my faith.

"Please, somebody, help my mum!" I scream. But no one comes. I desperately push the nurse call button over and over but it goes unanswered.

"Mum! Mum! Wake up Mum, please, wake up!" She is unresponsive. I run to the nurse's station just outside her door.

"Please, help my mum, there's something wrong!" I scream again. The nurses look at each other but they don't move. Instead they only look at me, then at each other.

"Please, she is burning up, it's really bad. Please! Why aren't you helping her?"

Finally the indifferent nurse with thick ankles gets up and walks across the hall to my mother's room. There is no urgency in her movement, and that pisses me off even more. *Come on, move faster, you useless woman.*

Inside the room the beads of sweat have formed into rivers flowing down my mother's face, now scarlet from overheating. She is unconscious. Her entire body trembles as boiling blood courses through her veins looking for an outlet. In any moment she will erupt.

"There's nothing we can do for her," the nurse says curtly. She turns to leave.

"Stop! Please, she's suffering, please. Do something. Please help my mother!"

"I'm sorry." The nurse leaves the room, closing the door behind her.

"How can you do nothing?" I scream at the door. "You're a nurse, goddammit! At least tell me what to do! Please!" I turn to my mum. "You're going to be okay, Mum. Just hold on, please hold on."

I pull the drenched sheets off of her, they are hot to the touch. I run to the bathroom and soak a face cloth with cold water. I place it on her head, but it instantly turns hot. Her body begins to convulse.

"Please, God, please, God, please, God. Don't do this. Don't you do this to my family again. I'm not ready."

I will not let you die. You cannot die. No. No. No. Screw the nurses, screw the doctors and screw death! The disgusting, untouched contents of her food tray smash against the floor. I take off running with the empty tray. Past the nurse's station and down the hallway, I reach the ice machine. The tray is trembling. I fill it with ice and take off running again. Seconds later I am back in her room, my hands are trembling so badly I can barely pick up the ice. I place it all around her head. It melts instantly.

I take off again, this time slowing down at the nurse's station. "Please help me! I need ice, please. Please!"

But they don't. They won't even look up. Back and forth. Tray after tray. I try to make an ice bath in her bed, but it's hopeless, it melts faster than I can put it there.

"Mum! Mum! Wake up! Wake up!" She won't wake up. I peel open her eyelids. If she could just see me, if I could just see her eyes, maybe she will wake up. I can't find her eyes. There are just bloodshot white pockets behind her eyelids. She is not going to wake up. Surrendering, I sit down beside her and squeeze her hand. My heart is being strangled, the slowest most painful strangulation. A huge lump in my throat threatens to cut off my breath. A pit of emptiness consumes my insides. I can't believe this is it. I'm not ready.

"Please don't die. Please don't die. Don't leave me. I can't live without you, Mum."

A voice comes from the doorway. "You have to let her go." The plump nurse with thick ankles is standing at the door. For a moment she almost looks concerned, as though she may care. She has never showed any emotion or compassion before. And if she cares, she would help my mother instead of sitting on her ass.

"Get out of here. You don't care! She's suffering, and you won't even help her! You walked out on her! On me! You are a terrible, terrible person!"

She sighs, but doesn't move. Why the hell is she standing there doing nothing? And why the hell is she telling me to let her go? This is my mother, *my mother*, dammit. She is not just a patient. She is my mother. And I am not ready to let her go.

"Help her! Help me! I'm doing this all alone. I can't do everything on my own! I'm all alone!" This is my mother. I can't let her go. How can I live without her? I love her so much. We have so many things to do together. We were supposed to go away for Christmas. And there are so many things I still need to tell her. This is all happening so fast. It's not fair.

"You have to let her go. She's in a coma. She's just holding on for you, dear," she whispers, unaffected by my outburst.

"Get the hell out of here!" I scream. "Never, ever come near this room again. You don't know anything and you sure as hell do not know my mother. She's strong, she wants to live, she is not holding on for me. And you have never been nice to her, even now! Get out!"

I jump up and slam the door before she can say anything further. My mother is purple. Her face and body is bloated with poison. The crystal heart necklace is now tight her neck; the chain is about to snap from the pressure. I undo the clasp and put it around my own neck. I lay down beside her, holding her hand as tight as I can and begin to bargain.

"Dear God, I will do anything, anything at all, if you spare my mother's life. You can have my arms, my legs, and all of my income for the rest of my life. Just please, God, please don't take my mum away from me. She is too young. I need her. She needs me. Please God. I will do anything, I promise, anything at all."

The wetness of the bed soaks through my own clothes, and I begin to shiver. I sob uncontrollably until exhaustion finally overtakes me.

14

How to Ruin a Crocodile's Day

"We gotta go," the Drill Sergeant says.

"What's wrong?"

"The croc pit flooded."

"What are we supposed to do — throw them life jackets?"

"No. There are no crocs in there right now. We gotta clear it."

The pit is heavily overgrown with reeds that are not allowing any natural drainage. Before the storm it wouldn't have mattered, but now the croc pit has transformed into a swimming pool. Our job is to go in and cut clear all the reeds, which should allow the pit to drain properly in a relatively short period of time. In other parts of the world, this job would be easily done with heavy-duty equipment, like a backhoe. But here, we'll use the ever-popular and versatile machete.

Ranger Frederick is waiting for us when we pull up. He is the reptile ranger, specializing in anything that creeps, slithers, or crawls. He is a welcome contrast to the Drill Sergeant. He has small, elf-like facial features surrounded by long locks of feathered hair — 1975 Farah Fawcett-style hair, and a polite disposition to match.

He speaks Afrikaans, but his accent is much subtler than the Drill Sergeant's. There is no harshness to his, and he doesn't make that strange *hhuucck* noise that the Drill Sergeant does.

Rastaman is already in the pit, slicing through reeds effortlessly, making it look easy. Rastaman's real name is Denver, but everyone calls him Rastaman because he is Rastafarian. He's quiet and keeps to himself; to this day, I've never heard him speak. I don't even know what language he speaks since here in South Africa, it could be one of dozens.

The pit is ten feet deep and overflowing with thick, straw-like reeds. In some spots, the water is high, but in others, it is just mud. Getting into the pit is like trying to get into an empty swimming pool with no shallow end, steps, or ladder.

Instead of making a fool of myself by attempting to get in this pit, I'll pass some time by taking some photos. This way, I can look occupied while I see how the rangers get in and out. They don't offer up any help though, they just leap in and out like frogs; it must come from years of practice. I'm not even going to attempt to do it the way they do, since it would only lead to one thing: disaster.

Frederick and the Drill Sergeant are in deep conference over the pit, trying to work out the best plan of attack, as though this is a complicated undertaking. It's pretty basic to me, it's nothing more than a glorified weeding job. There is nothing exciting about it. They both light cigarettes, which is my cue that it will be a while before anything happens.

This is the perfect time to make my move and attempt to get in the pit, while everyone is preoccupied. Perhaps if I go backwards and slowly lower myself over the edge, I can kick my feet into the mud to form a crude ladder. The idea's good, but on the first "rung" my foot slips and is unable to get a stronghold in the wall. I change legs and try the other one instead, but it yields the same results.

The rangers are still in deep consultation. They're probably just buying time so Rastaman and I will end up doing most of the work. I'll have to lower myself down as low as I can go and then drop; it's the only option. Later, I'll worry about how to get out of this dungeon of mud. It's a bit of a drop, but I make it without falling on my butt or slicing off an appendage with my machete.

The reeds are taller than I am, and I can't see the ground or anything below my waist. This is worse than wading through tidal pools of seaweed forests. This is Africa, so anything could be down there. What if there are snakes in this pit, swimming, poisonous, "thirty-five-minutes-until-death" snakes?

Don't look down. I am not waist deep in water. There is nothing in here. There are no snakes in here. What if there is a snake in here? Will I 'be able to ruthlessly chop it in half? Eeeeekk.

How do they know there are no crocs in here? What if there is a croc in here? They must have checked. They wouldn't send me in here if there were any chance a croc was here, would they? Maybe this is all part of the Drill Sergeant's plan. Maybe that's why he's pretending to be busy with the Keebler elf.

Stop obsessing.

I'm not obsessing.

This is a serious concern.

No, it's not. Just do the job and get the hell out of here.

I whack, chop, slap, and kung fu the reeds. Sometimes the machete slides off the muddy reeds, but most of the time it makes contact and cuts them down easily. With each fallen reed, my morale grows. Yahoo! I can't see anyone around me. The reeds are too high. Their presence is evidenced only by the familiar *ting* as their machetes make contact.

Soon, it becomes methodic and almost relaxing, and all thoughts of crocodiles and snakes have been chopped away. After a couple of hours, no reed is left standing. We rake and stack them into one massive pile of sludge. Another conference of cigarettes and Afrikaans slang is underway to decide what to do with the reeds. Do we load them into the trailer and take them to the dump? Do we just pull them out and leave them on the side of the pit? Maybe we should use them as filler to repair the roads.

The suggestion that garners the most support on this relatively boring, cold, and damp morning is to burn the bitches. That's right. The rangers decide the best course of action to take is to burn this wet pile of waste.

The Drill Sergeant strips a reed down to its core, flicks his lighter, and holds the flame to the frayed ends. After several seconds, it miraculously starts to burn. He turns it upside down like a match and crouches down. Leaning forward, he holds it deep into the pile of wet reeds. Is it going to spark? Will it burn? Is it just my imagination, or does the Drill Sergeant resemble a rhinoceros from behind?

All eyes are on the miniscule glow. No one dares to breathe for fear of blowing it out. Oh no! The flame disappears into a whiff of smoke. Cigarettes are lit for round two of the powwow.

The Drill Sergeant jumps, clapping his hands. "Yes!" They've had a stroke of genius. Frederick skips to the maintenance shed.

A few minutes later, he reappears holding a small plastic petrol pump dispenser and a large backup canister of fuel. He jumps down into the pit and ferociously pumps petrol over the reeds, soaking them. His blonde locks are tossed, his eyes are tiny slits and a giddy laugh escapes his lips. He looks like an elf gone mad, crazed with his petrol pump.

The Drill Sergeant is standing by, wearing a huge grin on his face. He strips another reed down to its core, lights it, and this time holds it in a petrol-soaked pile of reeds. Will this tiny flame grow into a raging fire, or will it just fizzle out like its predecessor? The rangers are determined to see its success.

They look like cavemen who have just discovered fire. Each one taking turns gently blowing on the flame, coaxing and willing it to grow. Drops of petrol are added—tiny drops, flirting with the flame, enticing it to ignite. Crack! Pop! The flame races across the reeds. The cavemen jump up and down, and their excited grunts echo through the pit. Snatching the petrol pump from each other, they fight for control to douse the fire with petrol, and each time the pile explodes into flames. *BRATATAT.*

The sky above becomes thick with black smoke that can be seen for miles away.

The small petrol pump is discarded for the big gun, the backup canister. Frederick dumps fuel directly onto the flames, transforming the pit into a blazing inferno. It's impossible to see anything through the smoke. Likewise, the air is polluted with burning dampness and the stench of fuel. Clean air no longer exists.

My nostrils are burning, and my eyes are tearing into blurriness from the fumes.

This doesn't slow them down, it only encourages them. They're mad, completely mad. More and more fuel is added to the fire. The rangers are out of control, drunk with adrenalin, each one of them fighting to hold the canister and the power it contains. *KABOOM!* The flames are thirty feet high. My skin feels like it may start bubbling off. *KAPOW!* It's out of control.

"Crocodeeeel, Crocodeeeeel!!!!" Rastaman screams at the top of his lungs—he has a voice, after all.

What? The Drill Seegeant and Patrick fight their way through smoke and flames to follow Rastaman's voice. Pulling my bandana over my face, I follow. There, in the corner of the pit, is Rastaman, holding up a clump of long grass with his pitchfork. Underneath of it, in a small primitive cave is a gigantic king crocodile.

"Holy shiiiiiiiiit!" Everyone screams in chorus once we realize the enormity of our actions.

"Get this fire out! Now!" the Drill Sergeant orders.

This entire time, I've been working in the thick camouflaged reeds, unable to see below my waist, unable to move faster than a snail, even dismissing my own legitimate concerns, there has been a giant fang-filled crocodile amongst us, and he is pissed. His yellow eyes are squeezed into slits, and his jaws are slightly open, ready to defend his territory. We have just destroyed his home right before his eyes. We could have just removed the reeds, but no, the cavemen decided to set fire to this king croc's castle, hammering it with endless rounds of petrol bombs, reducing it to nothing.

Everyone shifts into emergency mode. Rastaman tries to douse the fire by spreading reeds and stomping on them. Frederick has arrived with a hose and is standing on the edge of the pit, showering it with water. The Drill Sergeant is in the pit, trying to bring peace to what is now a war zone. Even Mother Nature has joined the firefight by pelting the ground below with giant raindrops. Despite our efforts, the fire is spreading quickly.

Smashing the burning reeds with a rake and stomping the flames into the mud, I keep one eye on the croc in case he bolts. But he doesn't. He isn't going to come out, is he? It's the perfect time to get a close-up photo of a crocodile. I'll never be this close to a crocodile again, while in a fire pit, with explosions going off all around me — this really is an once-in-a-lifetime opportunity.

I pull out my camera, zoom in on his fangs, and just as I snap the photo, the camera jerks as the mud swallows my feet. No one has seen me yet, so I can still take another shot without being seen and scolded. I take another shot, but upon reviewing the screen, I see that the smoke has made it blurry. This won't do.

Snap, snap, snap, I lean from side to side and forward with a newfound flexibility because my legs are heavily anchored in place. The mud swallows my knees.

Satisfied, I put the camera back in my pocket and pull my leg, only it doesn't budge. I pull again, this time putting my hand on the ground for extra leverage, but the mud quickly swallows it up as well.

Mother Nature has unzipped all the clouds above and in only a few minutes the once-puddles have now turned into pools. I may need help. Everyone's consumed with putting out the fire, which is almost out. I try again to pull myself out, but my legs won't budge.

The crocodile inches to the edge of his cave. Shit, he is coming out. The scent of my panic is too alluring for him.

Each time I try to dig my legs out, they just sink deeper. I look back at the croc and again, he has moved out further. Their strategy on land is to skulk and freeze, skulk and freeze, all the while their prey has no idea that the statue is getting closer, but *I* know he is getting closer. I have photographic evidence in hand of where he was just minutes ago.

That croc is going to get me. Frantically, I pull at my legs, they don't budge. I can't dig myself out. It's hopeless.

"Ha ha ha ha ha ha ha ha ha!" An elf-like cackle tumbles from Fredrick's mouth. Standing at the rim of the pit he drops to the ground in hysterics. What the hell is he laughing at? Why isn't he helping me? Can he help me without the Drill Sergeant noticing? Too late.

Standing at the mouth of the pit in front of me is the Drill Sergeant. He has come to rescue me. His face is stained black from smoke. His clothes are ragged and wet. His jacket has been discarded, and his dirty shirt is clinging to his muscular arms and chest.

I hate it that he can be so attractive. In this one moment he looks like a real firefighter, my hero — that is, at least until he opens his mouth. "What the hell are you doing taking pictures at a time like this? Serves you right if that croc snaps your arms off. Maybe that would teach you some common sense."

"Well who acted like a kamikaze with the petrol bombs? We wouldn't be in this position if you weren't a madman!" I scream.

"Well then, get yourself out," he says, turning away.

"Wait!" He wouldn't dare. "I need help, I'm stuck."

The Drill Sergeant's glare stains my cheeks red. Thank God they're masked in black soot.

"Come on then," he snarls.

Rastaman holds onto the Drill Sergeant's legs as he leans down, and offers me his hand. The pit has nearly flooded around me, it's too dangerous for anyone to get in. I take hold of his hand, and after a couple of powerful wrenches, he pulls me out. When my legs are free, he doesn't let go. Instead, he pulls me up the mud wall and drags me across the wet and muddy grass. Rastaman's laughter joins Patrick's.

Even through the thick black muck on his face, a dark purple shade of anger is visible. He looks more pissed than the now-homeless crocodile. I am a mud-covered fool. The crocodile survived, and was moved to another pit.

It took us eight hours to clean up what was left of that crocodile pit the next day. The Drill Sergeant never even uttered a word to me the entire time, but there was plenty of laughter amongst the rangers.

I hung my head low and tried to silence their laughter. I imagined I was in the middle of a war-torn country, parachuted in as part of an international rescue effort to rebuild this part of the world after man (rude, rhinoceros-butt caveman) had destroyed it so callously. It wasn't hard to imagine this while knee-deep in charred remains (even if it was only one rat), black soot, and slimy, fuel soaked muck. I tied my bandana over my face, forming a pseudo-oxygen mask that helped to eliminate the smell of poisonous gasses, but that didn't stop the pounding headache from the lack of fresh air. The sun had come out for part of the day, producing a hazy mist of condensation that transformed my fellow aid workers into robotic silhouettes digging and clearing the aftermath of devastation.

My cleanup tool was a pitchfork that was missing its center tongs. Each load I lifted was heavier than any dung ball of Kittibon's. In fact, the pit cleanup made the stable cleaning feel like a holiday.

15

Tree Planting

"Have you ever been tree planting before?" the Drill Sergeant asks.

"No but I'm willing to give it a shot." Sounds like a relatively clean job. It can't be any worse than the croc pit cleanup.

There's a break in the storm, but the forecast for the coming days is grim. It's the coldest, wettest winter on record in this part of South Africa. Clean-up efforts have been slow and difficult. Even getting around the reserve is challenging because road repairs have been suspended until the storm has completely passed.

"We'll just stop and fill the tire on the way to the lion camp," the Drill Sergeant says.

Harrison's left rear tire is near flat again.

"Lion camp?" I ask.

"Yes, that's where we're tree planting," he says with his usual air of indifference.

"Where will the lions be if we're in there tree planting?"

"In the camp, of course."

In the camp? *In the camp?* Just driving through the lion camp to deliver a carcass is a terrifying experience. Going in with a perpetually flat tire with the intention of getting out of the truck to plant trees — without a weapon, I might add — is just plain ridiculous.

"Maybe we should take Cruiser instead?"

"Cruiser is on another job."

"But the tire — what if it goes flat when we're in the lion camp?"

The Drill Sergeant huffs a dismissive sigh.

"Is anyone else coming with us?" The more rangers, the better.

"No."

Everything I have done up to this point now seems easy compared to this. Even tolerating the Drill Sergeant is easier than this. I'll do anything, anything at all, as long as it's not in the lion camp.

Since the storm hit, most of the wildlife has gone into hiding, but not the lions. The lions have been especially active since the storm, and their growls and roars can be heard all night, every night, even from within the concrete walls of the common area. They are charged up from the storm.

Reforestation of this land is a big part of the conservation effort. Hundreds of years of farming have destroyed most of the trees. However, reforestation is difficult and mostly unsuccessful for many reasons. First, there's no soil to speak of; it's just dried up, cracked, and hardened clay, an obviously inhospitable environment for planting. Secondly, there's the drought to consider. Saplings need lots of water to survive, so water has to be brought in. At the reserve, this is a method that is basically one step up from carrying it in a vessel on one's head. Water is transported in rustic containers that have been filled at the watering hole in a far corner of the reserve, then loaded into the back of a pickup truck, where it endures a long and arduous bumpy ride. Whatever's left by the time it arrives at its destination is given to the saplings.

Then, assuming the first two challenges have been overcome, there are the porcupines to consider, a sapling's greatest predator. Porcupines will go anywhere and do anything to feast on a sapling, including dismantling elaborate traps and maneuvering through intricate obstacle courses of electrical fences.

The anti-porcupine strategy the rangers developed over time has been to plant within the lion's camp. The strategy is not

100% successful, but the success rate is much greater with lions acting as natural guardians to the seedlings. It would take an especially courageous or insipient porcupine to attempt penetrating the lion's camp, and they sometimes do.

In order to deter these insipiently courageous porcupines, saplings are planted deep within the lion camp, far away from the border, reducing the porcupine's chance at claiming a prize, while increasing the porcupine's own chance of becoming a lion's prize.

Once the saplings grow into trees that can withstand a porcupine's attempts, the lion camp will be moved, and reforestation will begin in a new area until, eventually, this land is returned to its original habitat. The only downfall to this strategy is that somebody has to go deep within the lion camp to plant, and today it's us. This will be the most dangerous job yet.

We stop at the maintenance shed and load up thirty young trees. They're about thirty-six inches high and ten pounds each. After that, we make a pit stop to top up the air in the tire. The Drill Sergeant eyeballs the tire, not bothering to measure the PSI.

"Shouldn't you at least measure that?" I ask. How can he not take every precaution possible?

The Drill Sergeant laughs, tossing the air hose aside. He yanks open the driver's side door and the handle comes right off in his hand. He grunts and chucks it in the back of Harrison. Harrison is not the only one slowly falling to pieces this morning.

"It's an omen." Things are getting worse by the second, I have to get out of this.

"What are you talking about?" he asks.

"The flat tire, the door handle, they're all signs we shouldn't go in the lion's camp today."

"You're talking nonsense, woman."

"It's not just that. I have a bad feeling in my gut." I don't care if he thinks I'm crazy, I don't want to get eaten alive by a lion because of a flat tire!

"Probably just gas," he laughs as he jams Harrison into first gear. It's not gas, it's instinct, and it's never wrong. He is driving me into a certain death. How can I get out of this? I have all but demanded he take me back to the tent camp, and I can't exactly do that and keep some measure of pride. Stupid false pride.

Soon we're driving along the perimeter of the lion camp, outside the fence line. I strain my ears to hear any roars above the whir of Harrison's engine, but they don't come. The voracious carnivores are nowhere to be seen, either. Perhaps, by the grace of God, the lions are occupied with a porcupine and won't notice us when we come in.

We enter the first gate and wait in the holding pattern for it to close behind us. I try hard to release all fear and apprehension by breathing deeply and slowly. As soon as the second gate opens, my efforts are tossed out the window. My pulse quickens and my breath becomes shallow in anticipating what lies ahead.

Harrison loops around the long, muddy roads, going deeper and deeper within the camp. Now would be a great time for an urgent message to come over the radio, calling us away for a wildlife emergency. Please! Or even if the dark clouds looming above would just open up — that would be enough to pull us away from here. Instead it remains silent . . . and dry.

The Drill Sergeant parks in the centermost part of the camp, deep within a ravine, not far from where we deposited the carcass last week. I step out of the truck and look around. So far, no sight of the lions. Just a few feet away is the remnants of the carcass, nothing more than a skull, licked clean. Just off to my right, there is a cluster of sagebrush. It's not very deep, but it is deep enough for a lioness to hide in. She is probably watching me now, patiently waiting for the perfect time to pounce on me and rip out my spine the way she did to that zebra, without even breaking a claw.

The Drill Sergeant gives me a pick-axe to use for digging holes; its non-ergonomic design mirrors every other tool I've used. It's even heavier than the dung shovel. I practice swinging it overhead, should I need to use it to fight off a lion.

"Right, the quicker we do this, the quicker we can get out of here," the Drill Sergeant says, noticing my mounting anxiety. Shifting my attention to the task, I begin.

Even though it's been raining for several days, just under the surface, the ground is hard and brittle, making it tough to break through. On top of this, it's interspersed with rocks that send electrifying jitters up the shaft and into my arms each time I make contact. It takes a long time just to dig a small hole.

"It is hard to concentrate on digging holes when you have to look out for lions, isn't it?" Maybe the Drill Sergeant will agree and suggest we leave this job for the other rangers.

"Ah, by the time you saw her, it would be too late," replies the Drill Sergeant nonchalantly.

Soon paranoia makes it impossible for me to dig anymore. Instead I scan the horizon, waiting, watching, ready to run back to the truck. It doesn't take long until I spot something moving on the slope just above us, two lionesses.

"Look! There they are!"

"Ah yes, they've come out after all," the Drill Sergeant says and quickly turns his back to them. He is more concerned with digging the hole before him than the fact that there are predators closing in on us.

"I guess we'll have to come back another day, no sense in staying now," I say, trying to hide my relief at the prospect of leaving.

He regards the lionesses, "It's all right. We don't have to go anywhere. If they get within five hundred feet, then we'll get in the truck, but for now we're safe. They're just seeing if we have food."

"Seeing if we *have* food? We *are* the food! It's probably the smell of my fear that lured them here in the first place!" I shout, no longer trying to hide the panic in my voice.

"Just pretend they're not there," he says, losing his patience. "Let's finish this, so we can get outta here."

"But at five hundred feet that lioness would be here in less than three seconds! We should go, I mean it, I'm sorry but I think it's best if we leave and come back another day." Screw the false pride, I want out of here now.

The Drill Sergeant ignores my pleas like he always does. Instead, he continues to dig holes with his back to the murderesses. I, on the other hand, will not be so foolish. I will stand guard, and the second they move, I will alert the Drill Sergeant so we can get the hell out of here.

Oddly enough, they have taken a position near the fence. They appear not to be interested in us. I am not so easily fooled. Their plan is to make me comfortable with their presence, and just when I think it's safe to turn my back on them, they will pounce, and then it will be me lying on the ground, spineless, like that zebra.

My suspicions are right, for their voracious appetites are suddenly driving them forward down the hill, towards us. There is no male in sight; he must be waiting for the signal that lunch is being served before he bothers to get up. In the meantime, he won't expel any energy. He'll save his energy for ripping me apart, limb-by-limb. Then he'll gnaw through my fat in search of the meat that lies far below.

The dominant female holds her head high into the air and opens her mouth wide. She pants heavily as she smells the air with her tongue, tasting what's in her territory. I try hard to squelch my fear, pushing it down, far away from any of my pores or glands, so the scent won't escape and call attention to us.

My attempt is futile, for she is, at this very moment, leading the way towards us. She is not running; it would be too easy and too compassionate to end my life so quickly. Instead, she's moving slowly, one deliberate step at a time. Her muscular form skulks down low to the ground. She's not trying to hide herself because she knows I am no match for her. It's pure instinct that dictates her movements.

With each step, her shoulder blades roll back and forth in a rhythmic movement. Her eyes are in a trance-like state, fixed upon her target. Her mouth is still set open as it engulfs an appetizer of fear pheromones that are now running rampant from me. I want to scream, but I can't, my vocal chords are paralyzed in fear. I can't even warn the Drill Sergeant, who still has his back turned towards them.

She is well within the five hundred foot limit now. If she decides to run, she will be on top of us in less than three seconds; we have no chance of escaping her.

The truck tire has gone flat. We can't even escape if we wanted to. There is only one chance left, and that is to try and hide under Harrison and wait for help. I take a big step without thinking, keeping my eyes are focused on one thing, and one thing only; Harrison and the life-saving shelter he can provide. I dive underneath him with all my might, sliding to a stop just below the front axle.

The two seasoned hunters could drag me out of here. My thoughts are prophetic, for now they are closing in on me — one from each side of the truck — and there's no escape. Any second now, it will all be over, she'll yank me out by the leg. Her claws will dig into my thigh and slice through my skin like barbed wire. I'll try and push her head away, but my efforts will be futile as she rips my arm off from its socket. If she has an ounce of compassion, her jaws will be around my throat, piercing my jugular, and life will escape from me quickly. My screams, like a dinner bell ringing, will signal the male that it's time to eat. Is this the completion to my circle of life? Is this my contribution . . . to be lion food?

"Melissa? Melissa? MELISSA!" The Drill Sergeant's bellow jolts me back to reality.

"Huh?"

"Stop standing around — are you day dreaming over there or what?"

The lions!" My voice returns to me, I can now warn him that the hunters are moving in on us.

He finally looks up the hill. "The lions haven't moved." He shakes his head and turns back to the broken ground in front of him.

He's right. The lions haven't moved. They are exactly where they were before, lying, almost asleep, in the afternoon sun. I look over at the tire, and it, too, is still full, not flat, as I had imagined it to be.

How could I have imagined the whole thing? It was so real. I heard her. I saw her. Heck, I even felt her breathing on me just before she sunk her teeth into my throat.

Peter Pan declared that imagination, or a lack of it, is a mere reflection of a paradise lost — lost with age, with growing up. If, even for a moment, doubt can be silenced and imagination is free to flourish, then all things wished for and hoped for, or even those things feared, are suddenly within reach.

But sometimes hope fools us into believing that we can somehow change our current reality instead of just accepting it as it is. And when we try to change something that is beyond our control, something that is outside of our realm of understanding, we quickly set ourselves up for defeat.

"Melissa?"

"Mum!" She's awake! It's a miracle. My wavering faith is instantly restored and stronger than ever. They said she wouldn't ever come out of the coma, but she has proven them all wrong. They don't realize how strong she is. She's turned the corner just like I knew she would. She's going to be beat this monster.

Her voice is weak. "I love you."

"I love you too, Mum. Are you okay?"

"I'm a little tired."

"Tired? You were asleep for two days!" Overflowing with happiness, I nearly shout the words.

"What?" She seems alarmed.

I shouldn't have told her she had been asleep for so long. "Maybe it just seemed like two days. Are you hungry?"

"Yes, I'm starving."

"I'll go get some of that chicken you like from that place around the corner. What else do you want? Chocolate? Ice cream? You can have anything you want. Anything!"

"Chicken sounds nice. Can you put the TV on before you go, I'm afraid when you're not here."

"Of course. Don't be afraid, Mum, I won't be long."

"Please hurry."

"I will."

High on Cloud Nine, my feet barely touch the ground on the way to the elevator. Passing the other patient rooms, I want to tell them all to have faith—just look at my mum, she's going to be fine, and all the doctors and nurses were wrong, wrong, wrong. At least that is what I wanted to believe.

16

A Dual Between Logic and Fear

Tonight I am determined to sleep in my tent. I am ready to confront the demon of darkness and reclaim my territory. Tonight I will slay my fears, and be victorious. I am no longer afraid. Tonight I will sleep in my tent, I will, I will, I will. The time is now. I can do this. This will be easy. I can do anything, anything at all.

That was the mantra I was repeating over and over again earlier while the sun was still high. But now that the sun has set, there is an entirely different conversation underway in this black pit of pending death shrouded in canvas.

My face, previously sun-kissed by the crimson lipstick of the mid-day African sun, is now white, and its glow further illuminates the crepuscular gloom of my tent. Fear has painted my skin this color, careful not to leave any area exposed. The hair on my head, also unable to escape his reach, is standing on end, and goose bumps have flocked to my arms and legs, taking permanent residence there.

I've been "reading" in my tent for two hours, but am still on page one. My eyes are going through the motions, but my brain is unable to decipher the letters. It's too preoccupied with my ears, the dedicated troops that are delivering loud and clear the messages coming from outside.

Earlier, I made a lengthy inspection of all sheets looking for creepy crawlies, as I always do, and found nothing potentially deadly. But on this night, it's not what could be *inside* my tent that is bothering me; it's what's *outside*. The lions. They're extremely active, roaring and growling in an ongoing chorus—more so now than ever before. The wind is acting like an efficient courier, carrying their calls directly to my door, making it appear as though they're just outside, or perhaps they are outside. Perhaps the scent of my fear has brought them here at last.

The lions are taunting me, letting me know they can smell me. Even the wind is antagonizing me tonight, slapping the walls of my tent with ferocity like never before. I've been through this before; I thought there was a lion outside my tent and there was nothing, only wind. That's all there is now, wind. Or maybe this time it's real, maybe my luck has run out and there is a lion out there.

Breathe deep, relax, read the damn book. There is nothing to fear but fear itself. I repeat, *there is nothing to fear but fear itself. I will sleep in this tent tonight. I will sleep in this tent tonight. I will sleep in this goddamn tent tonight.*

Maybe it's mating season; that would explain why the lions are so lively and loud. If only I had a weapon, a weapon would make me more secure. If I had a weapon, I could sleep in this tent, no problem. But the only weapon the Drill Sergeant gave me was a headlamp. What am I suppose to do with that? Shine it in my attacker's eye?

RAAAAAAARRRRR. Oh, God! It sounds like the huntress is just outside of my tent. *There is nothing to fear but fear itself. There is nothing to fear but fear itself…RAAAAAAARRRRRRR. GASP! There is nothing to fear but fear itself. There is nothing to fear but fear itself.* Speaking the mantra louder and faster doesn't help to ease my nerves.

Get a hold of yourself! Somewhere deep within, an unknown voice speaks. *You're being crazy; this is absurd. Nothing is going to get you. You do this every time you're in this tent. Those lions are not going to jump the fence, why would they? Nothing like that has ever happened before.*

Oh yes it has.

Has it?

Yes, don't you remember?

No.

I heard someone, somewhere, not too long ago, talking about tourists being eaten alive by lions on a game reserve.

Really?

Yes. Come to think of it, maybe it happened here.

Wouldn't they have told me if it had?

Of course they wouldn't tell you. No one would come here if they told people.

I think you're right, I think I did hear something like that. How could I have forgotten something like that?

So why are you still in this tent...?

There's a long, excruciating pause as Fear and Logic square off in a duel of wits and will to see who will outsmart the other.

Finally, logic shoots: *Stop it!!!!!! That never happened, not here, you fool. The lions are not going to get out. Just read your book or go to sleep, and stop obsessing. You always do this.*

I try one last time to read, but it's hopeless. Maybe if I close my eyes, I'll fall asleep. I wrap the blankets over my ears to try and block out the growls of the lions. I try this, but after only a few seconds, I decide it's wiser to leave all my senses out in the open, so I can be forewarned of any dangers.

It's just then, as I force myself to close my eyes and try to sleep, that the wind, Fear's ally, slaps the wall so hard it nearly knocks me off my bed. With that, Fear seizes the opportunity and shoots back at Logic. I'm terrified to the core, and Fear claims victory in this duel. Logic retreats, defeated. *Perhaps it's better to vacate this tent, after all.*

Relieved that Logic is on board, I jump out of bed and prepare for the sprint to the common area. I poke my head out and scan my surroundings for the reflection of eyeballs that cannot hide from my light. There are none. The sprint lands me inside the common area in seconds.

I make my bed of tattered cushions and mummify myself in my blanket, trying to fall asleep quickly, while ignoring Logic's bruised ego. Screw the tent. There is no greater place than here, on the concrete floor of the common area.

17
Bribery in the Bush

"My cushions!" Magda screams as she yanks one out from underneath of me. "Why are my cushions on the floor?"

Dammit, I've become too comfortable in my slumbering transgression to the point of sloppiness. If only it had been someone else who found me in here, anyone, well, anyone other than the Drill Sergeant. Why did it have to be her, the camp mole and gossip queen? The African newsmonger herself has busted me.

She isn't even looking at me. Instead, she's madly inspecting the cushions for damage. She is furious that these tattered, ripped, poor excuses for cushions I used as a bed are on the floor. How does this woman make me feel like a six year old being scorned?

"I'm sorry Magda, I . . . I . . ." I don't know what to say. Do I admit that I'm a grown woman afraid to sleep in her tent? Magda is not afraid of anything, in fact, everyone's afraid of her. She'll scoff at the excuse of fear. What can I say to satisfy and, hopefully, by the grace of God, silence Magda so she doesn't spill my secret?

"I couldn't sleep in my tent, it was leaking. I was cold . . . and wet . . . it was uncomfortable."

It's hard to tell her a fib when her eyes cut through me, easily exposing the truth. The tents are of safari quality, able to withstand the most extreme and unforgiving heat, sun, and rain. Magda is no dummy, she knows this just as well as I do.

There is a long pause. Will Magda show me an ounce of compassion and keep my secret safe?

Magda or, Mama Magda as she is known around here, comes across as a sweet woman. She has a big, gracious smile, and her robust figure is always clad in the same frayed red apron, perfectly pressed and cared for in lieu of its flaws. She appears humble, a mere domestic presence who comes in a few times a week to cook and clean. But I see past all that, and can't be wooed by her mouthwatering meals of *baboti*, beef stew, and sweetbread topped with apples, like the rosy apples of her smiling cheeks. No, underneath that scarf-covered head is a mastermind whose dark, deep eyes hold many secrets . . . secrets of others, that is.

Mama Magda has several grandchildren, all who live with her in one of the tiny dwellings in town. The rangers are an extension of her already-huge family, and she treats them as such. It's not uncommon to see her running after a ranger swinging a rolling pin, and it's rumored she even whipped one of them once with a whisk.

She is the grand matriarch around here. With her self-awarded title, she demands not only respect, but knowledge of everyone else's secrets to empower her status as reigning queen.

She begins to laugh, a deep bellied roaring laughter that heaves and throws the many waves of blubber under her red apron like giant swells. I can't let her tell anyone, I'll never live it down. I'll be a laughing stock, and worse, the Drill Sergeant will know that every morning when I came out of my tent walking like a proud peacock, it was all an act, and that I was nothing more than a coward, a fake, a phony.

No longer concerned about her crappy cushions, she is bent over in hysterics, hugging her rolls trying to calm them. She knows my secret, and it's only a matter of time until she exposes me. But if there's one thing I know about finks and blackmailers, it's that they can be bribed, and this Mother Malefactor is no different. And so it shall be, I will engage in the old-age tradition of bribery.

I know exactly what will buy her silence. When I first arrived at the camp, Mama Magda had admired my British travel teapot.

She revered it like it was the royal jewels themselves. So, in a desperate move, I pick up my treasured teapot and present it to her.

She looks at me with surprise in her deep brown eyes, and I return her stare with eyes that beg for her silence. My treasured teapot has become a bargaining chip in exchange for muteness. She tries to refuse it, but I insist, forcing it into her fat little fingers.

We don't exchange any words but an agreement has been reached. Mama Magda accepts my pot, ensuring my secret is forever kept under the lid.

Mama Magda, just like Mother Nature, is a force not to be underestimated.

18
Holding on to Letting Go

"What's going on here?" the Drill Sergeant asks as he enters the common area.

"Nothing," I reply quickly, "Magda and I were just talking about the storm."

"Well, about that. Round two of the storm hit pretty hard last night. I know it's your day off, but I'm doing patrols and then some fence work if you want to come along."

"Sure." Anything will be better than being held captive by my tent all day, or worse, being in the presence of Mama Magda.

The wind carries a damp and bitter chill from atop the snow-capped Landberg mountain range down into the valley. Lashing my face through Harrison's open window, it penetrates deep into my bones.

"Are you sure there's no heat in this truck?" Leaning toward the dashboard controls, I flick random switches.

"Nothing works in here," the Drill Sergeant says while waving me back from the dash.

My fingers quickly go numb inside the once supple, yellow leather gloves that are now loose-fitting, hardened black sacs. The sky is dark, and the underlying mood in this valley is even darker. There are no signs of life anywhere. The valley is baron, lifeless and unkind.

"Where are all the animals?"

"Hiding."

The condition of the roads has worsened. Most of them have turned into rivers, but that doesn't stop Harrison from coughing and spitting his way through them.

Soon, we near the area where the sick hartebeest was seen a few days ago. *Please don't be here.* Her mate is the first thing we see. He is still anxiously pacing back and forth, even more restless now. He has been by her side for days protecting her from predators and reassuring her.

Maybe he tried to lessen her fears of dying. Maybe he told her that he loves her and will miss her, and not a single day will go by that he doesn't think about her. Maybe he reassured her that he'd be fine, that she need not worry about him.

However, even as he said those words to her, even as he reassured her it's okay to leave him, inside, he doesn't know how he will survive without her. Inside, he's scared. He can't bear the thought of being without her, of not having her to fall back on, to rely on, to love, and to be loved by her. He can't imagine a world without her, and he's terrified. Maybe he feels guilty that he can't make her better.

Desperately, I scan the area, praying she will still be alive and with great relief, I find her, alive. The Drill Sergeant pulls beside her this time and turns off the engine. She is in the same position as before, the coldness has hardened the mud around her body. Her eyes have lost some of their strength and her head is not so high anymore. I recognize defeat in her eyes.

I don't want to give up on her. She has to pull through this. She has to restore my faith that death can be slaughtered by hope and conviction.

Death, ugly, despicable Death, you will not defeat me here, I will not let you. I gave in to you once, thinking it would be easier to fold my hand, to acquiesce to you, but I was wrong. The pain only got worse when I gave in to you.

I tried to escape you, thinking I could run away, but you followed me to the other side of the world. You are a cold, heartless bastard. I will not let you win. I will not let you try to destroy me again as you did before.

I thought you had given up, but you tricked us. I believed she was better, I believed that she had turned the corner to a miraculous recovery, but it was your plan all along. You had an ace up your sleeve, and you waited until I was disillusioned by your deceit before you attacked, one final attack that would destroy my hope and crumble my faith forever.

I return to the hospital even more uplifted than when I left. I had called everyone I could when I was out picking up chicken to tell them the inexplicable story of my mum's recovery. She is the strongest woman in the world. I knew she would outlive us all.

My faith has been restored, but it won't last, for Death is finished bluffing and is now playing his hand aggressively to win. As I near my mother's room an indescribable horrendous sound overtakes the hallway. What is that?

The box of BBQ chicken hits the floor and explodes, sending pieces across the room. I can't believe the site before me. "What is happening?"

The desperate gurgling sounds are deafening. They're coming from deep within my mother's chest. The thick-ankled nurse places an oxygen mask over her face and cranks it up full blast. The combination of noise is piercing. There is terror in my mother's eyes as she fights for air.

"What happened to her?" I scream. "She was fine ten minutes ago!"

"She's drowning in her own lungs," the nurse says without looking at me.

"Drowning? What does that mean? Is she dying?"

"She's trying to," she turns to face me, "but she's holding on for you."

The gurgling noise is overwhelming. Control slips away and is replaced with panic. "What can I do?"

The nurse puts her hand on my shoulder, her eyebrows frown as she says, "Tell her she can go." She squeezes my shoulder, "I'm sorry." She quickly leaves the room and closes the door behind her, leaving me alone.

Regis and Kelly, her favorite show, the one that we watched together every morning in this room for the last twenty-two days is still on the TV. The audience laughs voraciously at one of Regis's jokes. Screw you, Regis.

It's one of those paralyzing moments when you realize you have disillusioned yourself into believing the unbelievable because the truth is too horrific to face. And now the truth is punching you in the face. Your life has changed forever, and there is nothing you can do to go back. Hope and faith are extinguished in one breath. Your prayers have gone unanswered, and there is not a shred of doubt that you are completely alone because not even God is listening.

I turn off the TV and take a seat on the edge of her bed and stare out the window. Everything is grey; the sky, the mountains, the buildings, and the streets—it all looks dead. So this is how it is going to be. Death's ugly grip is tightening. I have to stop resisting and take back what control I can by resigning to the reality I have been trying so hard to ignore.

"Mum?"

Her eyes are wide open but there is no response.

"Can you hear me, Mum?"

Nothing. I weep. Holding her hand as tight as I possibly can, I try to hold on to the strength and conviction I had moments ago. I have never felt so out of control, so useless, and so helpless. It is inevitable; I have to let her go.

I turn off the oxygen tank, quieting it. Leaning over my mother's ear, I begin:

"Mum, I remember so many good things. I remember the times you unexpectedly showed up at my ball games, standing in the bleachers with a bag of chewing gum for me. It wasn't very often but it didn't matter because when you were there, I felt like I could do anything. I was so proud when I hit the ball. But even when I struck out, it was okay because you were there cheering me on. I spent my entire third grade summer perfecting my mosquito repellent invention made out of compost.

"Looking back, I see how ludicrous it was, but you didn't; you wore the stinky repellent and pretended it worked. No matter how crazy my ideas were or how destined they were to fail, your words were always the same: go for it. You cheered me on my entire life, and whether I failed or succeeded, got battered and bruised, it didn't matter because you would be there to pick me up and remind me to never stop trying.

"You always just knew when something was wrong, and you knew how to make me feel better. Your strength never wavered in all the storms we went through. You were committed to your family, and we never went without. You have nothing to regret. I know how much you love me, and I love you. I always will. You are a good mother, the best mother I could have ever wished for."

I wait for any kind of an acknowledgement that she hears me, but other than her gasps for air, she is still. I swallow hard, but each time, the lump in my throat grows bigger, I can't speak. The tears are streaming down my face. I have to say it. I have to let her go.

"You can go, Mum."

She tries to speak but she can only gurgle. I will never hear her voice again. Hope and faith will never be reignited. I am finally letting her go. There is no going back.

"I will be okay, Mum. You can stop holding on. Just let go. Let go, Mum. Please let go."

I feel her hand flinch. She wants to yank it out of mine. It is the most movement in her hand since the night I found her on the floor at home. Disapproval, anger, disappointment, I feel it in her hand in that moment. It cuts through my heart like a dagger, leaving it heavy in guilt. She is not ready to give in. She still has the fight within her, but without me by her side, she can't hold on. The strength that she relies on within me is no longer there. I have surrendered to Death. I have accepted his triumph and told her to do the same.

Her eyes blink and a tear rolls down her cheek. Guilt and failure consume me. I want to embrace her to beg her not to go, but I can't, I have to free her and myself.

I quickly stand up and walk out of the room, firmly closing the door behind me. I am in a trance. My whole body and mind are numb. I take the elevator down to the main level. I walk into the cafeteria, but never sit down. I don't know what to do with myself. I am lost.

I end up outside in the bitter cold air. The mountains are socked in with ice clouds, but they don't look nearly as cold as I feel inside. I cross the street and slide behind the wheel of my car and wait, staring straight ahead.

Eventually I put the key into the ignition and turn over the engine and pause again. I take one last look up at her window on the 6th floor. What have I done? From the outside, it looks peaceful, the twinkling lights and the Christmas decorations. But inside there is a battle going on and defeat is imminent.

19

Mending Fences

"Can you feel that?" the Drill Sergeant asks.

"What?"

"There's something in the air. I can't really explain it. It's like the air is new, like the storm has washed it, but there's something else. I feel . . . something."

"I feel that this weather sucks." I thought Africa would be hot and sunny; I didn't expect rain and near freezing temperatures.

"Effervescence," he blurts out suddenly.

"What?" How would the Neanderthal know a word like effervescence?

"There's a certain effervescence out here. Do you feel it?" he asks again, smiling.

"Do you even know what effervescence means?"

"Yes I do. Do you feel it?" he asks impatiently.

"No."

"It must be all this cold air, I'm not use to it."

I am feeling something, too, but it isn't effervescence. What I'm feeling is something much more sinister than mere excitement. It's epicurean, and it's obviously stemming from my vulnerable state after seeing the dying hartebeest. How dare I even feel a hint of these vile feelings towards HIM? This weather isn't helping either. He looks different since the storm hit. He hasn't shaved in a few days "to keep his face warm" as he says.

He looks rough around the edges with that five o'clock shadow, making me want to see him after five o clock, if you know what I mean. Ugh, vile thoughts! With rigid jaw and full lips, he's the South African version of Grizzly Adams. It's not just his overgrown facial hair that's changed. He's traded in his summer uniform for a winter digs: a khaki rain jacket that has Ranger printed in bright yellow letters across the shoulders over a khaki fleece. He even wears a khaki wool cap—there's something barbaric and animalistic about it. Ugh! I *must* fight off these feelings for that Neanderthal. "What are we doing today?"

"Pulling down a fence."

"Seems like you pull down a lot of fences around here. We pulled down that big one last week."

"And we'll be rebuilding it next week," he grumbles.

"What?"

"We pulled down the wrong fence last week. Today we'll pull down the right one."

"Wait. You got us to pull down the wrong fence? Ha! How did you manage that?" I can't believe it. Finally the Drill Sergeant has screwed up. We spent nearly an entire day pulling down that fence last week.

"Paperwork was mixed up."

"Well, I think it's hilarious that you had the crew pull down the wrong fence! Too bad I won't be here next week to help you rebuild it, ha ha ha!"

"It's almost as funny as you sleeping in the common area every night isn't it?"

What? How the...? Damn Mama Magda. I curse her for disclosing my secrets and for breaking the international code of honorable blackmail by playing both sides. She has a teapot to return, and I will make damn sure she does so as soon as I get back to the camp.

"I see you coming out of there every morning from across the camp. You didn't know that, did you?"

The tops of my ears threaten to burn off.

"It's no big deal. You're not the first volunteer to sleep in the common area, you know." He sounds compassionate, and from the corner of my eye, he looks more handsome than ever.

"Don't take this the wrong way . . ." he starts.

Oh my God, is this the moment when he tells me he also knows of my nickname for him? And that he, too, has one for me? I've seen him looking at my butt in the elephant stable. He probably thinks it resembles the back-end of a rhinoceros, or maybe he thinks I look like a distant cousin of Kittibon from behind. His nickname for me is probably something like Wide Load, or Big Bertha. Or perhaps he just calls me BB, short for Bubble Butt.

Or maybe it is not my butt. Maybe he's going to tell me he finds me attractive, too. Does he?

"I must say that you are the hardest working volunteer I've seen here," he says.

"Pardon me?" I don't know if I should be pleased or disappointed.

"You've worked hard, and yes, you've pissed me off enormously at times, but overall, you've stepped up to the challenges. I thought you'd be long gone to Cape Town by now."

I don't quite know what to say. I guess if it can rain in this drought-laden part of Africa, then it's not too far of a reach for the Drill Sergeant to give me a compliment.

The only thing I can muster is, "Thanks."

We drive the rest of the way in silence . . . again, until we reach the lions' camp where several other rangers are already busy at the fence line.

"The lion camp?" Not the lion camp again.

"Yes. There's an old perimeter fence around the lion camp beside the other one, and we've got to take it out."

"I never saw another fence." I can't believe we have to work beside these bloodthirsty predators again.

"It's right beside the camp perimeter, just a few inches outside of it, hard to see unless you're looking for it."

I step out of Harrison into the tall blonde grass just outside the lion camp. My feet sink about six inches in the mud. I yank my foot out leaving my sneaker behind. The rangers begin to roar with laughter.

"Come on everyone, let's do this," orders the ever-impatient Drill Sergeant.

There's a bit of scrub brush in between the two fences, blocking the view into the lion camp. The fence was part of the old farm that was here before the reserve was built. It's made of wooden posts spaced fifty feet apart with four rows of barbed wire running the length of it.

We spread out and begin dismantling the long fence. Using needle-nose pliers, half of us pluck out the rusty staples from the posts, releasing the wire. Each time someone pulls a staple out, there's a *toing* sound that echoes down the wire, followed by a vibration, *toing, toing, toing*. Once the wires are out, another ranger comes along and kicks down the wooden post.

Rustle, rustle, rustle. Why is the brush rustling? What is that? *Rustle, rustle, rustle.* Holy shit, it's the lions.

"Aaaahhhhhhhh!" I scream. While trying to run away, I slip in my wet sneaker and fall backwards onto my butt.

Everyone freezes, and all eyes are staring down the fence line; they must know it's there, too. The Drill Sergeant makes his way towards me. He should be running. Why is he stopping to kick down a post on his way here? Doesn't he realize that there is a lion about to jump this fence? *Rustle, rustle, rustle.* Wait a second. He kicks down another post, which is followed by another rustling noise. Oh my God, it's not a lion making that sound, it's just the wire scratching the scrub brush each time a post comes down.

"What's wrong?" he asks.

Now I have to think fast. I cannot tolerate any further humiliation. "There was a huge spider on my hand," I stutter.

"How big?"

"It was almost as big as my hand. It jumped on me, from that bush. It was the biggest spider I've ever seen."

"Really?"

"Yes and it had big pinchers, almost as big as these pliers." I hold up the pliers in front of my mouth opening and closing them like deadly pinchers. The lie is growing with each word I speak.

"Did it bite you?" he asks, concerned.

"I don't think so. I flicked it off before it had the chance."

"Incredible."

"It was a huge spider, with giant pinchers, the size of these pliers," he shouts down the line, as he holds up my pliers.

"A huge spider . . . giant pinchers . . . pliers." My lie is echoed down the line, as each ranger shouts it to the one behind him.

"Anyway, it's gone now," I say quickly.

"What color was it?"

Why won't he go away? Why is there an inquisition over a silly spider? Who cares what color it was? Everyone knows there are flesh-killing spiders here. I'm not telling them anything new.

"It was brown," I answer.

"Light brown or dark brown?"

He's relentless with his questions. Why does it matter? I reach for my pliers from his hand. "Light brown."

"Like the color of sand?" he asks, pulling the pliers just out of my reach.

"Yes, like sand," I agree, trying to appease him so he'll go away and take the spotlight off of me.

"It was the color of sand!" he shouts down the line, and again the lie is echoed by each one of the rangers.

"Did it have bent legs like this?" he says, bending his elbows up to his ears and shrugging his shoulders.

"Yeah, I think so. It all happened so fast, I don't really remember." Now I'm getting agitated. Why won't he just give me my damn pliers back?

"It was a violin spider!" he shouts down the line.

This time, as the echo makes its way down the line, one by one the rangers come running towards us.

"Violin spider! No way! Amazing! Where is it?" Everyone shouts over each other, scrambling to get to the front to see the imaginary spider. Machetes are drawn and bushes are hacked away in search of the spider that doesn't exist.

Once again, karma is instant in the bush, for my lies keep me in the lions camp for an extra hour while the rangers smoked cigarettes and pow-wowed about the significance of this species that has never before been seen in this area.

20

Birth of an Understanding

"She's dead."

"Are you sure?" I can't look at her. Instead my eyes are fixed on her partner standing on the hillside, watching her.

"Yep, she's dead."

The Drill Sergeant gets out of the truck to examine the hartebeest.

I didn't know Death was going to rear his ugly head today. In fact, I never expected him to follow me halfway around the world. I thought I could evade him by crossing two continents and putting 20,000 miles in between us. But Death doesn't know boundaries like time and space. It was naïve of me to believe I could run away from the son of a bitch.

Death doesn't give a damn about anyone else's feelings. He's unpredictable. He's ruthless. A thief of innocence, he forever steals the twinkle out of an eye — the twinkle that disappears once those eyes see Death up close and personal. He doesn't care about the ones left behind, the ones who have to deal with the impact he has left in his wake, the loneliness, the grief, and the uncertainty. He leaves no answers, no reasoning, and no promises — only a lingering feeling of shock, emptiness, and sadness. He's a powerful entity who, despite my protests and hatred for him, is always close by, waiting for me to let my guard down. And when I do, the heartless bastard sucker punches me in the gut, leaving behind a big ugly empty hole.

I can no longer contain my own memories of Death to the blackness of the night or the boundaries of my tent camp.

~~~

"She's gone," the nurse whispers as I enter my mum's hospital room.

Death has overtaken the room, filling it with a stale and desolate stench. I look toward her bed, but my eyes stop just short of it. I can't see her like this. Instead my eyes settle on the steel table where gold-rimmed spectacles are neatly folded. Near them, a brown wig cut into the style of a mushroom cap. The Cancer Society had given her the wig just three weeks after the aggressive chemotherapy treatment took her hair away. We had laughed about the wig's resemblance to a mushroom. She hated wearing it, not just because of the style, but because it made her head hot and sweaty. I had reassured her that her golden curls would return one day, and this was just a minor setback. And that was what I believed. Until this very moment, I didn't believe it would ever come to this.

She was such a strong woman. Her Viking roots made her tough, but her life made her even tougher. She couldn't be intimidated by anyone or anything, not even cancer. She would beat it, she said, and I never doubted that she would. But it wasn't just her strength that made me believe she could overcome this disease. It was the games the disease had played. When attacked with drugs and radiation, it made itself weak, even hiding at times. It had fooled us all.

"The tumor looks good on the CAT scan," the doctor said.

"What do you mean?"

"We've never seen a tumor shrink this much, so fast. This is incredible."

I became hopeful. "Does that mean the cancer is going away?"

"It's positive news, but cancer is unpredictable. We'll scan her lungs again in a few months."

"Can she go away for Christmas?" I asked. "She has always wanted to spend Christmas on a beach in Mexico."

"If she feels up to it, sure. There's always a chance that the cancer has already metastasized, but so far, it looks really good."

"What does metastasized mean?"

"It means spread. Lung cancer is aggressive, and it can metastasize to the brain very quickly."

"How will we know?"

"Sudden paralysis, stroke, pain. Those are the most common symptoms."

"Can you do a scan now to see if it's already metastasized?"

"No, we wait until three months after treatment has ended. Early in the new year we'll bring her back in."

"Are you sure you can't run any tests now?" My uneasiness is noticeable.

"Go to Mexico, spend Christmas on the beach, and we'll see you in the New Year." The doctor was so reassuring.

Eleven days later, I would find her paralyzed on her living room floor. We would spend the entire night waiting for a non-emergency ambulance. She would never go home again.

Hope, optimism, even miracles came and went during the course of this disease, but in the end, it was Death that prevailed.

"I'll give you some time alone with her," the nurse says, making her way towards the door.

My heart crumbles. Shivers cover my body, sending my hair on end. The emptiness is overwhelming. Pushing past the nurse, I leave the room without ever looking at my mother.

"Pass me that cable," the Drill Sergeant shouts.

"What?"

"I said pass me that cable . . . the winch . . . on the truck. We gotta move this hartebeest outta here."

"Where will we take her? What will happen to her?" Why is he being so abrupt, an animal is dead. Can't we take a moment?

"She's cat food now."

"Cat food? Shouldn't we bury her, or . . . something. She deserves something."

"Circle of life—her death is another animal's dinner. We've talked about this before. Are you going to help me, woman, or not?"

"I can't." I'm paralyzed just as I was in the hospital. I can't bring myself to look at the hartebeest.

"You can't be afraid of death. If you fear death, you fear life—it's the same thing."

"I'm sorry, I just can't do this."

"If you were afraid of death you wouldn't be here, in Africa, would you?"

He's right. Death is part of life and in avoiding dealing with it, I'm avoiding life. I have to confront it. Now.

I force myself to look at her. Her head is slouched forward, her lips pressed into the mud. Her giant, black eyes are vanquished and void. I can't pull my eyes away, if only I had not been such a coward before. Now it is too late. Cremated and cast away at sea, my mother is forever gone.

It was a fatal mistake on my part to believe that Death was something that existed outside of me, for when confronted by him again, he completely consumes me. He overtakes me from the inside, where I had made a comfortable home for him. I am too exhausted to run anymore. Instead, I stand before Death, and succumb to him. And as I finally let go of my fear of Death and allow my wound to be exposed, something totally unexpected occurs.

My enemy is not who I think he is. He somehow becomes less evil and less intimidating. He has lost all his power over me—the power I had given him.

The Drill Sergeant kicks the hartebeest in the side with a hollow thud and a small stream of urine trickles out of her. He cinches the cable tightly around her neck.

"Turn on the winch," he orders.

I move the switch and, as it begins to turn, her neck snaps back from the force. Her partner watches from up on the hillside. Motionless, he keeps his vigil until she is loaded into the truck.

Then he turns slightly to look at me. We seem to look right into one another as an unspoken understanding is reached. But there is one major difference between he and I; he stayed until the very end. He did not let fear or guilt drive him away. He is stronger than I am.

With one leap, he is gone over the hillside, never to be seen again.

21

One Victory

I'm on top of the world this morning, like I can conquer anything. I'm elated, unstoppable, and positively radiant with courage.

The reason for this newfound mojo that is bursting from my seams is that I, single-handedly, on a solo mission of determination, have killed the Boogieman. I defeated him with the stealth of a Ninja, the resolve of a Viking, and the sleekness of a hired assassin.

It's true, I have slain the dragon of darkness once and for all. I am no longer forced to live in exile because I have reclaimed my country and become a national hero — even if that country's borders are my tent walls, and I am its only citizen. The tent that was once a temple of doom is now my castle, my solace — my home.

Last night was the first time the silence was silent. There were no mystery noises, no whispers, and no ravenous beasts at my door.

The previous evening's weekly ranger's meeting in the common area went late. I was waiting in my tent for them to finish so I could sneak back in. Their meetings don't usually last more than half an hour, but last night's meeting was long, since it included plans of reconstruction after the storm.

The last thing I remember was opening my book. And then the next thing I knew, I was awakened by the squawks of the Hadeeda. I did it. I slept in my tent. How can I not be positively ecstatic?

The storm has finally passed. As I wait for the Drill Sergeant to pick me up, my senses feast on a smorgasbord of delicacies. My eyes devour the sky above as the artistic genius magically fills his canvas. The near-black backdrop just above the mountain peaks comes alive with brushstrokes of pink, lavender, and purple. This is followed by the faintest touch of silver wisps that yearn for the sun's reflection to bring them to life.

I feel alive just watching it all come to be; I am finally one with this land. I have survived the outback, and the Drill Sergeant. I have embraced it in its entirety, no longer crippled by the unknown, by the darkness and the sounds it whispers in the night. No longer afraid of Death.

Harrison rolls up, and I climb into the back. The Drill Sergeant raises an eyebrow at me, but even his disapproving gestures can't rattle me today.

"What are you so happy about?" he asks.

"Can't a person just be happy?"

I carefully place my feet on either edge of a big rusted-out hole and cast aside any physical flaws Harrison may have. For now, a new vision of Harrison is forming before me, a vision more appropriate for this fine victorious morning.

His chipped and dented body becomes a Roman chariot, gleaming white with gold embellishments. My crappy gloves, stained with blood, dirt, and soot, are now long, golden gladiator gloves. A pair of powerful white stallions with flowing silver manes has replaced Harrison's fatigued 275 horses under the hood. I hold on to the roll bar tightly as if it is a pair of reins. His mighty stallions take off into a rumbling gallop. I hold my head high as the ruler of these lands, the heroine who has defeated the demon of darkness. On this bright and glorious day, I am welcomed by a sea of loyal subjects . . . well, not so much a sea as just two: Bonty and Wildebeest.

"Good Morning, Bonty!"

Bonty's big satellite ears turn and twitch as he looks up.

"We did it, Bonty! We did it!"

During this experience in a distant world of sleepless nights, wild beast confrontations (that includes working with the Drill Sergeant), combative elephants, and confrontations with deep-rooted beliefs, we are triumphant at last.

This was supposed to be a mission of giving, but the more I give of myself, the more I receive from this place and all its inhabitants.

It is no coincidence that my neighbor is this little outcast in white knee-high socks. Bonty inadvertently reminded me of a truth that had long since escaped me: I am never alone.

"Good Morning, Wildebeest!" I call out, as we pass by the other lone grazer.

His beard is no longer grey but, instead, is covered in brown mud, and although it may not have seemed possible, he looks even stranger than he did before.

The Drill Sergeant has acquired an old boom box that's now sliding around on the dashboard, beating out sweet sounding tunes. The timing is perfect on this victorious day.

"Turn it up!"

The Drill Sergeant turns it up, and although it's crackly and fades in and out, I can make out the song, and nothing is more suitable on this fine morning than the words that fill the air:

"We are the champions my friend, and we'll keep on fighting till the end. We are the champions, we are the champions, no time for losers, 'cause we are the champions . . . of the world . . ."

It's one of the greatest songs of all time, and even though the radio can barely be heard, I'm belting out the words at the top of my lungs, and I don't give a damn who hears me.

My chariot comes to an abrupt halt.

The Drill Sergeant leans out his window. "Would you kindly shut up, Madam? We are looking for buffalo, and your screeching—that I dare say is worse than a Hadeeda—will not exactly entice them to come forward."

Yeah well have you seen your butt lately? Cuz if you had you'd probably think you were looking at the rear end of a rhinoceros. If only my castle had a guillotine.

"Why are we looking for buffalo?"

"Deworming. Have you ever de-wormed a buffalo?"

"Of course not. And why do we have to de-worm wild buffalo?"

"Storm, all the moisture, it's precautionary," he says matter-of-factly.

The Drill Sergeant stops the truck and gets out of the cab. In his hand is a large syringe. It is nearly as long as my arm. What am I supposed to do with that? Do I have to sneak up on a buffalo from behind and . . . oh, disgusting, I can't do that! Maybe we inject them by mouth? But how does he expect me to get a syringe in a buffalo's mouth? Maybe I'll have to inject it subcutaneously into a layer of muscle. But where, and more importantly, how do I do that? What if I get pulverized into smithereens? I won't do it. I refuse. I don't have to do anything. This is preposterous, and tantamount to mutiny!

The Drill Sergeant climbs up into the back of the truck and begins separating piles of Lucerne.

"You can't make me do this," I say stubbornly. "It's a little out of range you know."

His voice is tinged with his usual annoyance. "What are you talking about now?"

"You can't make me inject a buffalo. I will do most things, but I am not going to do that."

"Well do you think you can inject a pile of Lucerne?"

I blink. "Inject Lucerne?"

"Yes, Lucerne."

"Well I didn't know, I . . ."

"When the buffalo come, throw one bundle to each buffalo. Think you can handle that?"

I nod.

"Are you ready?" asks the Drill Sergeant, who is now comfortably back in the cab of the truck, smoking a cigarette.

I draw out the medicine and quickly inject each stack. We wait, but there is no thundering of hooves, no ambush from the sagebrush, no buffalo to be seen or heard. We wait in silence.

I try to think of something to say but nothing comes to mind. I could tell him about my victory, but he'd think I was trying to prove something to him. I could tell him why the death of the hartebeest affected me, but we don't have those kinds of conversations. Heck, I'm just finally starting to understand him. And he's all over the place; one minute he has incredible insight, and the next he's acting like a Neanderthal. He's too complicated. I can't understand what he says half the time, anyway.

"Here they are," the Drill Sergeant whispers. "Wait until the first one gets here, then start throwing it. Only one stack per buffalo."

The first buffalo races up to the back of the truck, catching me a bit off guard. I try to throw a heap past him, but he ducks and weaves in perfect sync with my moves, and I can't get it past him. He's getting frustrated waiting for me to throw it, and so is the Drill Sergeant.

"What the hell are you waiting for?" the Drill Sergeant yells.

"I, uh, well, he won't move."

I throw a pile at him quickly to avoid further insults from the Drill Sergeant, but the dang buffalo tries to catch it. The pile gets stuck on his horns. He is still trying to shake it off just as the next buffalo arrives. I lean forward with my rake to try and knock it off his horns.

The Drill Sergeant puffs on a cigarette, and watches in disgust. "What the hell are you doing with the rake? Throw the Lucerne!"

I throw the next pile at the second buffalo, but the first bull gets to it first. I have to get the stack off his horns so he doesn't eat the other one's food. I try to use my rake again, but am quickly surrounded by buffalo.

The second bull tries to eat the Lucerne off the first buffalo's head. The first buffalo takes it as an assault and charges back. I throw another pile to try and break up the fight, but this just causes more chaos. The third buffalo takes a head butt to the rear from the second buffalo that is running away from the first. The Drill Sergeant flicks his cigarette out the window, shaking his head.

I throw another pile, far away this time, to try and separate the gluttonous beasts. I continue throwing piles quickly, and as far as possible.

Observing the frenzy that is taking place, it is obvious that our strategy — or maybe just my execution of the strategy — is not going as planned. Each buffalo is eating the other's Lucerne. The first buffalo is still wearing his dose instead of eating it, and the fattest one seems to be eating everyone else's. He's probably going to overdose. The Drill Sergeant's face is now a light shade of purple.

I laugh. "How *do* you de-worm a buffalo anyway?"

"It's a lot easier than the final jobs I have planned for you before you leave us," the Drill Sergeant says through clenched teeth.

22

The Chase

It has only been two days since the storm has passed, but already the mud is hardening and the ground returning to its former parched state.

The wildlife has come out of hiding. Herds of springbok, a few hundred deep, are seen leaping across the weary roads as a new energy fills the air.

The ellies frolic in their watering hole that is now overflowing in mud. Selati rolls in the luxurious brown goo, and appears to be smiling. Even Kittibon looks happy.

The hormonal rhino is quick to get back to work, trotting around his territory in muddy breeches and a muddy snout marking the perimeter to keep out trespassers.

The giraffes stand together chewing in rhythm, as though nothing has happened. The storm's only lasting effect on them is knee high socks of mud.

Today we're driving a real game drive safari vehicle. Poor old Harrison is back in the shop again. We're perched in my favorite spot, the upper ridge, where we can see everything below in the valley. The Drill Sergeant and I never speak much, so it's a given when we sit at this spot that we won't disturb one another with idle conversation. That is at least, until today.

"There's a good game on tonight. South Africa's playing—8 o'clock," the Drill Sergeant says unexpectedly.

"Oh."

"Do you have any plans tonight?" He asks while looking out the windshield.

What *plans* could I possibly have? Tent reorganization? Laundry in the camp sink? Haggling with Mama Magda?

"No."

Still looking out the windshield, he mumbles, "Well, if you want to come and watch the game, I could pick you up."

What's going on? Is the Drill Sergeant asking me on a date? I have never felt more awkward than I do right now. Why the hell do we have to be having this conversation here—in our peaceful place—where I never have to worry about trying to make small talk? And after all this time, now he decides I may want to get out of my tent camp and socialize?

A twig snaps. The brush rustles. The Drill Sergeant holds his finger up to his lips, motioning me to be silent. Thank God for whatever it is. One more minute of this awkwardness, and I'd puke. The noise grows, but ever so faintly. The source of the sound is moving towards the edge of the brush.

She eventually reveals herself, a female Kudu. Kudu are easy to find on five star menus, but not so easy to find in the wild. They are timid and elusive, especially the male, thus earning him the nickname, the Grey Ghost.

They usually travel in herds of females with one male at the center. When they move, the females always lead the way, ensuring the safety of the male, who will not move until he knows it's safe. I've never seen a male kudu in the wild.

Male kudu are extremely powerful. They can weigh up to six-hundred pounds and have massive antelope horns that can deliver a thrashing to predators or other male kudu trying to overtake their herd. Their greatest defense though, is their hearing. Their big round ears are five times as sensitive as a human's, picking up sounds we can't.

Today is my last chance to try and capture the grey ghost on film before I leave the reserve.

Another female emerges, shortly followed by another one. They are leery of us, but continue anyway. Any moment now, the king kudu should appear. The camera is aimed and zoomed into the opening where the females are still coming out. I won't take any chances of missing him.

A pair of massive twisted horns appear, they can only belong to him. A face covered in black and white war paint peeks through the brush. He pauses. His round ears rotate searching for danger. I instinctively hold my breath. His stance is tall and regal. My God, he's gorgeous.

He edges forward an inch at a time, ears shifting back and forth. His shoulder span is massive, and he's twice as big as the females. *Keep coming, I've almost got all of you in the shot.* Another inch forward. *Keep moving, that's right.* He pauses. He's almost in full view, but it's close enough. My finger barely squeezes the capture button. *Wait, why is he…?* Oh no, click, click, click . . . he's gone! He bolted! What happened? Did I get him? Please! I review the screen, but it only reveals blurred grey images— similar to that of a ghost.

Hissssssssssss, hisssssssssssssss. What the…? A seven-foot tall, two-hundred pound poultry alien is charging us. His knees are bent backwards, and his long toes claw forward in long strides. His pink, bald bulbous head swings back and forth on a long, prickly neck. Jagged teeth protrude from a wide yellow beak; he is the ugliest creature on this reserve, or for that matter, anywhere.

"Here we go!" the Drill Sergeant shouts.

The ostrich just manages to kick the truck in the rear as the Drill Sergeant leaves him behind in a cloud of dust.

"What is his problem?" I ask.

"Mating season. He's loaded with testosterone, and more aggressive than the rhino."

"What an ugly bird!"

"And dangerous. That ball on the front of his head is a deadly weapon, and you don't want to be on the other end when he swings that thing."

"Ick. And he ruined the photos of the kudu. I got nothing but grey blurs."

The Drill Sergeant has a laugh. "Congratulations, you have captured the grey ghost on film!"

I laugh, too.

A few minutes later, a voice comes over the radio, shouting something in Afrikaans. The Drill Sergeant answers quickly, and pulls a U-turn, flooring the gas.

"What is it?"

"Buffalo has been spotted where they're harvesting thatch reeds. We gotta go over there and lure him away from the workers."

"How are we going to lure him out of there?"

"We'll have to piss him off," he says, returning to his air of indifference.

How does one piss off a buffalo?

We arrive at the area where the workers are huddled together, machetes in hand, looking very relieved to see us. They point to the direction the buffalo was last seen. It is dangerously close to where they are.

"Drive," the Drill Sergeant commands while jumping over the seat into the back.

I haven't driven right-hand drive other than the near-escape from the elephants a couple of weeks ago, and that was in Harrison. This supercharged engine, snorkel exhaust, and gargantuan tires is a real safari truck, and it's a monster compared to Harrison. Despite its lack of doors, windows, or even a windshield, it still feels like a tank.

I feel like I'm piloting a covert military operation as I take my position behind the wheel and jam it into first and accelerate while slowly releasing the clutch. Putt putt putt. It almost stalls, so I floor it through the rough ground. It takes off like a bullet. I push in the clutch again and drop it into second, and this time the transition is flawless. I've already mastered this thing by the second gear.

"Yee-ha! This is awesome!" I shout.

The Drill Sergeant shouts out directions from the back of the truck. It's hard to tell what's road and what isn't in this area, since it's all sand. The tank pulls through sand pits with no effort at all; it can take us anywhere. This is better than awesome; this is totally awesome.

"Look out, Mr. Buffalo, 'cuz here I come! Yeeeeee-hhaaaaaaaaaa!"

The Drill Sergeant cuts me off. "Stop yelling like a baboon, and slow down. I see him."

I push in the clutch and tap the brake until we nearly stop, then slide the stick back into first.

"Cut the engine," he whispers.

I do so, but there is still no buffalo in sight. '"Where is he?"

"Right behind that clump of reeds, just behind us."

I turn around and sit up high on my knees. I barely make out the top of his boss.

Buffalo have a massive black chunk known as "Boss" at the base of their horns. It resembles a 1960's men's hairdo parted in the middle that's been slicked down on either side with black grease. From this angle, even at 1,500 pounds of solid muscle, with that funny hair do, he hardly looks like Black Death, as buffalo are often referred to. But the Drill Sergeant assures me that when pissed off, buffalos are capable of goring (a.k.a. pulverizing) any African animal to death — even a lion.

Even when injured by a hunter, these beasts have been known to ambush and kill the very hunter who injured them in the first place, earning them the label of most dangerous hunted animal in Africa. Buffalos kill an average of two hundred people a year — more than all of the Big Five combined.

The Drill Sergeant pulls a knife from his pocket. What is he going to do? Throw a knife at the buffalo? Anticipating the worst, I watch and wait for him to launch the knife. Surely there must be another way.

The Drill Sergeant leans forward and slices the rope off a bundle of Lucerne. Phew. He throws a bunch of it towards the buffalo. The buffalo edges forward, from behind the reeds, and devours it.

He snorts and charges the truck. I don't wait for the Drill Sergeant's command, I'm already turning over the engine. I am meant for this kind of work. Never before have I been more in my element. Danger is my middle name and pissing off buffalos is my game.

"Drive, but not too fast, we want him to follow us."

"Okay."

"Stop riding the clutch."

"I'm not riding the clutch. Stop telling me how to drive."

I push in the clutch and gear down to first. Where is that buffalo? There's no rearview mirror, but a quick glance over my shoulder verifies he is right on our tail.

The Drill Sergeant drops another handful of Lucerne. I stop as the buffalo eats it even more voraciously this time. As he looks up for more, I push in the clutch and drive on again. It's a game of chase, with the buffalo tailgating us.

The Drill Sergeant makes short, quick huukk noises, mocking the buffalo, which just antagonizes him even more as he chases us. He's gaining on us. His snorts are louder than the pounding of his hooves on the ground as he pursues us.

Let's see how fast a buffalo can run. I push in the clutch and drop it into second, speeding up only slightly. He picks up his pace, too. I push in the clutch and shift it into third, speeding up even more, and throw in a couple of quick turns, just for fun.

"Slow down, we're losing him, for chrissakes!" the Drill Sergeant shouts.

I drop it down into second and then roll it into first. The buffalo is no longer in sight. I have been successful in losing him, but that was the opposite of our mission. Shitballs. I cut the engine and look back hoping he finds us again.

And out of nowhere, there he is, and what a hunter he is! He's charging us at full speed, how could we expect anything less from the most dangerous animal in Africa.

I twist around while simultaneously turning the key. I push in the clutch, shove it into first, and accelerate, but the tank doesn't move.

The Drill Sergeant shouts the obvious. *"Go!"*

I push in the clutch again and give it another burst of gas, but the tank remains motionless. I look over my right-hand side through the gap that would normally be a door and see that the front tire is deep in sand. I look at the back tire, it, too, is deep in the sand. The Drill Sergeant pounds the back of the truck. I push in the clutch again, and this time I jam the stick into reverse. Maybe I can rock this tank out. Failure. No movement except for the buffalo who is closing in on us fast.

His impatience is about to explode. "What the hell are you waiting for? Drive, woman!" he shrieks,

"We . . . uh . . . oh boy, how do I say this? The thing is, we may be stuck, sort of . . ."

"*What?*" he screams, as he turns around to glare at me.

"We're stuck," I say a little louder this time, without looking at him, but bracing myself for the rear-end assault from the buffalo that will be here any second.

"Move!" he shouts, while vaulting over the seats and landing almost on top of me as I feebly try to move over to the passenger seat. "Get in the back!" he screams.

Why do I have to sit in the back and be the first point of contact for the bull?

"Throw some Lucerne. As far as you can!"

I frantically throw Lucerne in all directions in my best attempt possible to distract the raging buffalo.

The 1,500 pounds of raging flesh arrives. Is he going to gore me to death? Not yet. He dives into the Lucerne.

After several minutes of trying to rock us out of the sand trap, the Drill Sergeant finally manages to get us out. It's a good thing, as I have just finished feeding the eating machine the last of the Lucerne.

The Drill Sergeant wastes no time in delivering me to the tent camp. We don't speak the entire way. I am too embarrassed, and he is too angry. He parks without turning off the engine. I jump down from the truck, when he unexpectedly asks, "Are you coming to watch the game tonight?"

The awkwardness returns. Is it just me that's being weird about this? It's just a soccer match, that's not a real date, is it? What would be a real date out here? A picnic beside the mud pit? Cocktails in the elephant stable? Maybe it is a date. Lately, he has fleeting moments of humanity. He's not *always* an ogre like he was before. I feel myself becoming weak, vulnerable, attracted . . . to him. The way a moth is attracted to a light in the dark, only to be burned.

"No, I don't think so."

Potential disaster is averted. My tent is the safest place for me to be. How the tables have turned in the last few weeks. My tent is a safe haven? I find myself attracted to the Drill Sergeant? Melanie would never believe it.

A few more days, and we will be reunited in the bustling city of Cape Town. While I'm sure she's having a fabulous time, the city now seems like a foreign place to me. I have gotten use to being out here in the bush, and have long since given up most modern day conveniences. They're useless out here. Survival is more important than having moisturized skin or flawless hair. Nourishment of any kind tastes divine when physical labor drains every ounce of energy within. I use to be a picky eater, but now I'll eat anything — and enjoy it. Things I once held sacred have become insignificant. I balk at the importance I ever gave things like matching luggage and impractical shoes.

But more than the material things I have managed to let go, it is the unseen that this place has freed me from: fear, doubt, death, uncertainty, and loneliness. Stuck in the middle of nowhere with no distractions, no underlying buzz and hum of a city, everything is coming into plain view.

23

Rumble with the Rhinos

"You want each one to be about this size," the Drill Sergeant says, while holding up a rock the size of a lime.

He is still happy over South Africa's victory last night. Thankfully, the sand pit incident has been forgotten.

Before us is a mountain of rocks of all different sizes — some are small pebbles, and some are as large as watermelons — all have sharp and jagged edges. This is our road-rebuilding material, and the tools to be used are nothing more than our hands.

One by one, I toss the rocks into Harrison's back end, smashing and cracking as they land, adding more dents and holes to his pitted bed. We have to move thousands of rocks to fix the road that was decimated by the storm. With all my twisting and tossing, it doesn't take long before the small rocks feel as heavy as the big ones. We've only been working for fifteen minutes, and I try to calculate how much longer it will take us to fill the truck, since it feels like it must be halfway full by now. I don't dare to look at our progress because I know we've got a long way to go.

I need to take a break before I collapse, but I will need an excuse to stop working. It kills me to do this, but the burn in my back trumps the awkwardness of a conversation with the Drill Sergeant. I take a seat on the bumper and conceal my relief as my muscles begin to relax.

"So, do you have a girlfriend?" I ask. As soon as I say it, I want to kick myself. *Who cares if he does? What a stupid question. Now he's going to think I want to know, like I'm curious or something.*

"No," he says.

"What do you do on your time off?" *Another stupid question; what's wrong with me? He's going to think that I actually care what he does with his time or, heaven forbid, he may even think I want to occupy some of that time.*

"Hunt."

"You protect animals for a living but hunt them on your time off? That doesn't make sense."

"I hunt to eat, not for sport."

"What else is there to do around here?"

"Nothing."

"Is there anywhere to go shopping, or to a movie? Is there a pub around here?"

"Not really."

"So what do you do, then? For fun?"

"Not much."

"Do you ever say more than two words?"

"What?"

"You just seem kind of quiet all the time. Other than blasting orders at me, you don't say much at all."

"I just am what I am. I'm me. I don't pretend to be anything I'm not. I'm not a show-off, I'm not a big talker. I don't have to act, I don't care what anyone thinks, and I don't have to BS anyone."

"Okay, but you have barely said anything to me in a few weeks. I don't even know anything about you, and we work together twelve hours a day."

"You want to know me? Okay, fine. Let's see. I don't have any money. In fact I make barely enough to get by, that's why I hunt for food. But I love what I do for a living. I'd rather do this than get paid big bucks to do a job I hate. That's all. What else do you want me to say? If you want me to pretend I'm something I'm not, I won't. I don't need to impress you or anyone else. Everyone's busy trying to pretend they're something or someone, or that they're better than the next guy. That's not me. Not very impressive is it?"

I don't know what to say, I was just trying to draw out a break, not open a can of worms.

This entire time the Drill Sergeant has been Mr. Quiet, Señor Dud, Monsieur Aloof, and Master No-Personality. The guy rarely speaks, and when he does, his words leave me speechless. First, it was his profound attitude about death, now this honesty about who he is and his disregard for what society's bullshit expectations are. Maybe he is human after all.

I nod my head in agreement and begin tossing rocks again. The pain in my back has disappeared, along with my previous beliefs about the Drill Sergeant being sub-human. He's not as much of a Neanderthal as I once thought he was.

When the truck is finally full, I climb in the back, this time balancing myself upon the rocks. I see him looking at me through his side mirror. I'm looking at him, too.

We arrive at a section of road pitted with grooves so deep that even the game vehicles could easily snap an axle if they attempted to drive this route. They're full of mud at least four inches deep.

The Drill Sergeant reverses to the edge of the first deep groove. It's going to take several truckloads. Crap. Nothing is easy in this place.

"So, what do we do now?" I ask.

"The main thing is to make sure you lay the rocks flat so no sharp edges are pointing up, otherwise they'll pop a tire."

The Drill Sergeant throws the rocks down to me, while I place them like bricks, careful not to let any sharp points stick out. This work is a lot easier than the load up. I'm working as fast as I can to keep up with the speed in which he's throwing rocks to me. He tosses the rocks just outside of the grooves, so they don't splash me with mud.

"How come there's no machinery here to do this?" I ask.

"In South Africa, we do things the way they were done a hundred years ago."

"That's obvious, but why?"

"Because we have no money."

I never thought I'd be rebuilding a road by hand. It's hard work, but healthy work. There was a time when I may have thought this kind of work was beneath me, but not now. Now, I am rising up to the new challenges that are given to me each day.

"Ouch!" I shout, while gripping my finger, trying to snuff out the sharp pain from a stray rock thrown by the Drill Sergeant.

"Sorry about that," he says with a cocky smile.

Soon we're back in the rhythm of placing rocks. I'm completely engrossed in placing a particularly difficult stone when I hear the Drill Sergeant let out a long slow whistle. He'd better not be looking at my butt again. I look up, but it is not my behind he is whistling at. Just a few feet in front of me, in between the truck and me, are the mama and baby rhino.

"Stay put," he whispers.

The little hairs on the back of my neck stand erect. "What do I do?" I whisper, without letting my lips move.

"Don't panic. Just relax."

Easier said than done when there are a couple of tons of horned prehistoric beasts beside me.

I've failed at one of the very basics in survival training when working on a reserve, I let too much distance get between me and the truck, and I'm in a crouched position, making me appear weak to the wildlife. If I try and make a run for it, it will look like I'm challenging them. Instead, I have to be assertive without appearing intimidating. I'm not supposed to move or make eye contact. I'm screwed.

My thighs are burning and cramping. Beads of sweat are forming on my forehead. My hands are sweating inside my gloves. My mouth is dry. My breath is fast and shallow. My body, against all my conscious internal commands, is showing every sign of anxiety possible, instead of behind relaxed and assertive.

The mama rhino breathes heavily through flared nostrils, creating puffs of swirling dust. She stomps her feet and shakes her head back and forth. Her rage is building. She is about to erupt. Her three-hundred pound baby mimics her, stomping and huffing and puffing. Little shit. The Drill Sergeant will save me; he always saves me. Why the hell isn't he saving me?

Rhinoceros have poor eyesight, they're almost blind, and rely heavily on scent, instead. If I throw some rocks in the other distraction, as per Melanie's technique, I may be able to distract them long enough to get away.

My idea comes too late. The rhinos rush. I cover my head and the ground stirs under the weight of the dusty duo. I can't run even if I want to because my legs are cramped, and the pair is too close. The rhinos storm past me just barely out of arm's reach.

The Drill Sergeant is shouting from the back of the truck. "Run, get in the truck, go, go, go!!!"

I can't move. *Damn you, legs, MOVE*!

"Get up, woman!" he shouts again.

"I can't, my legs won't move."

"You have to stand up. Move. Now!" he shouts louder.

I pry my legs up and against all odds began to run towards Harrison.

When I reach the tailgate the Drill Sergeant grabs me from under my arms and pulls me into the back of the truck. I scramble over the rocks to the cab of the truck to catch my breath, and look for the rhinos.

It is not me the rhinos were charging. On the opposite side of the road is the hormonal male, and in their ongoing turf war, Mama and Baby are chasing him—not even noticing, or perhaps just not caring that I was crouched down in a gulley before them.

I give myself a once-over. My legs feel like overcooked noodles, but I'm otherwise unscathed.

"Why don't we switch for a bit?" the Drill Sergeant says, jumping down to the ground, "You look like you've seen a ghost."

"That was incredible, they came out of nowhere. It happened so fast."

"Yeah, I've never seen anyone turn so white so fast before," he laughs as he begins placing the stones.

"No, I mean it. That was incredible. I'm not afraid anymore . . . of anything!" I'm filled with pride.

"You got lucky. It was chance, nothing to do with skill," he says easily.

I throw the rocks quicker and he places them just as fast — it's quickly turning into a competition. I carefully choose a large stone and wait for the opportune moment when the Drill Sergeant is completely distracted and unsuspecting.

Plop, splash, the rock lands in the mud puddle right below the Drill Sergeant's face and splatters him from forehead to chin with mud, dripping from his eyes and the end of his nose.

The Drill Sergeant doesn't even wipe his face. Instead, he whips a handful of mud and it splats right in my open, cackling mouth. My laughter is cut short as I spit out the grit that is stuck in the back of my throat and on the front of my teeth.

"It was pure luck you didn't get trampled!" he shouts.

I choose another rock, this time bigger, and again smack it down into the puddle just below him, walloping him with another splash of mud. "It wasn't luck, it was skill!" I shout back.

This time, I laugh with my mouth closed, as I anticipate another handful of mud will soon be cannoned at me, and it is, accompanied by the Drill Sergeant hollering. "Luck!"

I pick up a few rocks and throw them in quick sequence, spraying bullets of dirt while yelling. "Skill, skill, skill!"

He fires back, this time scooping handfuls of mud at the back of the truck. I jump down, and with both feet I dive into the pit, soaking both him and me. We both stomp our feet, splishing and splashing until we are covered from head to toe in mud, both of us in hysterics. Every time a mud bomb explodes, tension is released, and with each layer of mud that covers him, a layer of the Drill Sergeant's tough outer shell is shed, and he becomes more human.

Seeing him covered from head to toe in mud makes me want to get even closer to him. He is becoming more and more irresistible by the day. It takes every ounce of control I have not to throw myself at him instead of the mud.

24

Running with Bulls

Harrison speeds down the highway in a haze of noise pollution. The rickety old trailer in tow rattles as the thousands of pieces of wire bits holding it together are stretched to their extremes with every pothole. Patrick, the ranger who resembles a Keebler elf, is in the back of Harrison, holding on for dear life with his eyes squeezed shut to prevent a hair whipping injury from his long blonde locks.

I look back at him, and then at the Drill Sergeant. "Shouldn't we let him in?"

"Nah, he's fine," he says, shrugging off my concern.

The sun is high, and the sky is a brilliant hue of baby blue. The mountains reach far beyond the reserve's valley, extending nearly as far as the Indian Ocean a few miles away, which is where the great white sharks live.

Clink, clack, rattle, bang! The railroad tracks at the entrance to town nearly rip our caboose apart.

"Slow down, I want to really see everything this time. Last time, you flew through town."

"We don't have time, we're bringing back a double load of branches. Nothing to see here anyway."

"There are people to see," I say just as we pass a group of teenage boys, "Good Morning!" I shout from the window.

They are startled. One hollers back something in Afrikaans. I don't know what it means, but when he says it, the Drill Sergeant pulls his cap down lower over his face. One even throws a stone at the truck.

"Hey!" screams Patrick.

Patrick covers his head to protect himself from a hailstorm of rocks launched from the group of laughing boys. His cursing is muffled by the *bang, crack, toink,* as rocks bounce off of Harrison's already-battered body.

The Drill Sergeant steps on the gas, and again we're speeding down the road.

At the edge of town, we turn down a dirt alley. It is not the same way we went before to cut branches. There are no proteas lining the sides. Instead, it is heavily overgrown with weeds.

"Where are we going?"

"There is a farmer's field down here, where the branches are bigger and better," he says.

Bigger branches?

The narrowing dirt road becomes rougher and bumpier; it doesn't even look like a road anymore, even for South African standards. We turn another bend, and ahead is an old gate made out of chicken wire. This must be the back door to the farmer's field.

When the Drill Sergeant stops, he can't even open his door to get out because we're so thick in the overgrowth. Patrick climbs over the front of the truck, instead, and pulls back the fence, dropping it onto the ground.

Harrison edges forward, barely squeezing through the small opening. When we come through the other side, we're greeted by a mob of waiting bulls. They surround the truck, making it nearly impossible for Harrison to pull forward. They are territorial and don't like us being in their field. These bulls are aggressive, and some are even scratching the ground with their hooves. The Drill Sergeant honks the horn, but it doesn't dissuade them, and they continue to block the road. Each time he inches forward, it aggravates them further. Finally, he revs the engine and floors it, creating a wake of legs kicking everywhere as they scramble to get out of our way.

The field is rough and full of potholes and shallow ditches, putting Harrison through hell. The trailer squeaks, squawks, and shutters over each obstacle, but stays in one piece, defying basic engineering principles. The bulls are following closely behind — the whole herd of them. A quick count puts their number at about forty.

Harrison stops at the edge of a line of massive trees. There are no skinny trees here, and I'm not going to be able to chop down one of these trees, not even after three weeks of boot camp in the bush wielding a machete every day. The Drill Sergeant and Patrick leap from the truck and shimmy up the giant trees, holding machetes in their teeth. They leave me sitting in the truck that is now surrounded by bulls.

I open my door, but the ringleader charges me before I'm even out. I slam the door just before we're intimate. "Go away!" I shout through the open window.

Nobody moves. The ones at the back of the pack just move in closer, pushing the ones at the front against my door. The one beside my window has huge horns. I swear they're bigger than my machete.

I overhear Patrick talking to the Drill Sergeant. "Those bulls are getting pretty aggressive. They don't want to let her out of the truck."

"She's okay," the Drill Sergeant says with a smirk on his face. "She says she's not afraid of anything,"

There's fear, and then there's stupidity. "Can someone please help me?"

"No, you'll be fine, you can manage — use your *skills*," the Drill Sergeant laughs.

He is just as stubborn as these bulls. Well, they may be strong and stubborn, but they're not smart. I can trick them. If I just open this door and pretend I'm coming out . . .

Yes! They fall for it. In one swift movement, I slide across the cab and bolt out the other door. I run around the back of the trailer, but hadn't really thought of what to do once I got out. The pack is closing in. I must get to higher ground, fast. I climb up the side of the rickety trailer . . .

"Eeek! Oh my! Ah! Back off, you bullies! Leave me alone! Eeeeeeeekkkkkkk!"

"Are you going to help us, or just play with bulls all day?" the Drill Sergeant shouts.

"Perhaps someone could distract them, or . . ."

"No, no, you're brave enough. You're not afraid of anything, remember? We don't want to get in your way. Carry on."

Bastard. I look for a clearing and leap from the back of the trailer. As soon as I hit the ground, I hear the thunder of hooves behind me. I sprint for the closest tree and reach for the lowest branch. I try desperately to pull myself up as my feet run up the side of the tree trying to find some traction, but it's hopeless.

"Hurry up then! You're wasting valuable time over there," the Drill Sergeant shouts again.

I drop my machete and beeline it for Harrison, flailing my arms and screaming. I scramble up the hood and over Harrison's face onto the roof. The bulls, however, are not behind me because they have long since lost interest and disappeared into the forest. How long have I been running around like an idiot?

Patrick is laughing so hard he nearly falls out of the tree, and I've never heard the Drill Sergeant laugh the way he is now.

I can't even climb up one of these trees let alone chop their massive branches. I resume my previous important position as branch collector.

"I hear you're going to do the great white shark dive when you leave here," Patrick shouts down at me.

It's not true. They're trying to make fun of me. Up until now I would have never even considered such a ludicrous idea. But, on the other hand, why not do it? Why not face a lifetime phobia and silence it for good? If I don't do it now, when will I? I've never had so many close encounters with wildlife as I have here. My confidence is at an all time high, so why not?

"Yes, I am going to do it."

"You *are*?" they can't hide their shock. Now who's laughing?

"Yes, I am."

25

Khaki Fever

One of the least talked about, but most dangerous diseases native to South Africa, is Khaki Fever. Visitors to this country must take heed, for this disease is selective, in that the locals are immune to it, but thousands of visitors fall victim to this precarious and often-serious condition every year.

There is not a lot of information available about this disease. Suspiciously, it is not even listed on the World Health Organization's website. Perhaps victims will lobby for a change in the future, encouraging open communication of this potential epidemic. I sure hope so.

As far as I know, there have not been any reported cases of Khaki Fever outside of this continent's borders. If there have been, then I am quite certain they are not nearly as bountiful as they are here. Sure, there's Uniform Fever, but it is not anywhere near as dangerous as Khaki Fever.

The origins of this disease are unknown, but one may surmise that the earliest cases were a few hundred years ago, during colonial times, when the first settlers made South Africa their home. Those brave settlers lived off the land and had daily confrontations with wild and dangerous animals, facing fear with unsurpassed courageousness.

After these pioneers, more adventure-seekers came for a taste of this wild continent they had read about in letters or newspapers, in which photos emerged of grand, hunted animals never before seen.

When the newcomers arrived, they were overwhelmed by the ferocity of this country, the purity and harshness of it all. They found adventure, but their adventures couldn't have happened without a guide, a guide who became their safe-keeper, the one who kept them alive and who showed them a new life they had never been privy to. It was during those early days of discovery that the first cases of Khaki Fever came to be.

Not much has changed since that time. People still come to Africa seeking adventure, and they still get infected with the fever.

The fever is contracted from the very ones who guide them and keep them safe; the rangers themselves. The disease has evolved over time, with the evolution of women's roles as wildlife guides and rangers, so it's no longer just women who are afflicted by this disease, but men as well—men who find themselves in the hands of a rifle-bearing woman clad in khaki slacks.

This indigenous and elusive disease cannot be easily avoided, often incarcerating the most unsuspecting victims. There are no warning signs. One moment, the individual is fine, and the next, she is completely engulfed by this foreign, feverish state that has been appropriately named Khaki Fever, for khakis are a necessary ingredient to bring the fever to fruition.

What makes this fever so lethal is that, to this day, there is no known cure; one must simply wait it out until it passes. During this cooling-off period, one must exercise every ounce of willpower and strength within to not allow it to overtake her senses and sensibilities, forcing her to do something that she may deeply regret later.

The fever's symptoms are similar to the common fever:
- Cloudiness in judgment.
- Inability to think clearly
- Poor decision-making skills
- Excessive sweats and a general feeling of 'warmth' all over
- Flushed cheeks
- Goose pimples

- Trouble sleeping
- Light-headedness producing uncontrollable giggles and laughter at things that are not funny to anyone else other than the victim

New symptoms that have arisen from this khaki-provoked condition that are different than a common fever include:
- Daydreams that can be promiscuous in nature
- Pangs of passion and lust
- Aching that seems to be emanating from the heart and/or the groin region
- A fixation on a particular ranger that is far more than a mere crush
- An overwhelming tendency to flirt, giggle, blush, and act like a fool in love
- Pedestal Syndrome, in which the victim places the ranger on a towering pedestal
- Blindness, in that she cannot see the obvious faults in the ranger, and instead sees perfection where it does not exist
- Hallucinations – the individual actually believes that the feelings of love and passion are mutual, or worse, real
- Superhero Syndrome – the ranger is no longer seen as human, but, instead, is seen as a superhero
- Unbridled libido

The fever comes on suddenly, when the unsuspecting victim suddenly finds that she is attracted to a ranger, one whom, in otherwise normal circumstances (i.e., if they were not in the middle of wild Africa) there would never, *ever*, be the slightest physical or emotional attraction. Said victim even may normally be repulsed by such debauchery with said ranger.

Typical victims include tourists who have come for safari, or volunteers who have come to volunteer on a game reserve and who suddenly find themselves with an overwhelming feverish passionate desire for the ranger with whom they are in contact every day.

The rangers are aware this condition exists, and although it is seen as a serious condition to the foreigner, the ranger looks at it in quite the opposite manner. The ranger sees it, not as a disease, but as an inevitable condition caused by his masculinity and fearlessness that inevitably draws females to him.

This is the reason there has been no attempt to find a cure or even vaccination for a condition that elevates egos in some, while simultaneously crushing it in others.

In very rare cases, a person suffering from this illness will have to be removed from the vicinity and returned to a city at once, far away from all shades of khakiness. It may take a few days, but eventually the fever disappears and normal life resumes for the individual.

I have not fallen victim to this fever. I am one of the lucky ones. Granted, there have been times when, from a distance, under extreme duress or fatigue, that I have thought the Drill Sergeant attractive. But I have always been quick to shrug off that ridiculous notion. I mean, this disease clearly only affects the weak and vulnerable, and I am neither, not at all, and I am sure that the temptation would have to be great . . . and, well, there is not even the slightest temptation for me . . . really, none at all. That would be absurd.

I would have to be suffering some type of head trauma to feel the slightest bit of desire for him. He is still, in my humble opinion, a close relative of the Neanderthal, who merely exhibits fleeting instances of humanity.

This Khaki Fever has not and will not take hold of me . . . I am nearly certain of that. Okay, dammit, that was before. I hold the hormonal rhinoceros culpable for the first real signs of fever I am experiencing today. It's not my fault. If I was of sound mind and body, this never would be happening, but it's that damn rhino and his hormonal flare-ups causing mass destruction that are the cause of my imminent condition.

It was this morning, while on our morning patrols, when the call came through on the radio, the call that would set my case of Khaki Fever in motion.

There's one watering hole on the reserve that is fed by an underground spring. It's hard to believe that such a thing exists in this destitute dry patch, but it does. The watering hole is not only used by the wildlife, it's also used as a grey water source for the reserve operations. The water is pumped to a main distribution pump house and distributed from there.

It goes without saying that the pump system, like everything else here, is archaic. There's one long pipe that's hooked up to a diesel-powered pump that sits on the bank of the shore. Nearby, is a gas canister, which someone uses to re-fill the generator every 24-hours, or so. Without the pump, there's no running water here. All water depends on this one antiquated pump that is exposed to wild animals, including the belligerent rhinoceros.

This morning, the male rhino, suffering a temporary fit of hormonal rage, decided to thrash the pump and accompanying main pipe. When we arrive at the scene, there are two young, inexperienced rangers trying to fix the problem. Even I can see that they appear to have no idea what they're doing. Their blank expressions say it all, even as they hold tools in their hands and look at the mess of miscellaneous parts strewn across the muddy bank.

The Drill Sergeant looks at the mess the rhino has left behind. "Silly old rhino is frustrated."

The rhino isn't the only one who's frustrated.

The Drill Sergeant doesn't waste any time assessing the situation. He leaves me sitting in the truck and begins shouting orders in Afrikaans. The rangers hang on to every word he says, as though he is a great intellect or something. He's pointing his arms here and there, wrenching tools from their hands, and stomping about like a Napoleonic general.

He's wearing black rubber boots that make it easy for him to maneuver on the muddy bank. The young rangers are wearing tennis shoes and sliding all over the place as they run around trying to fill his orders. It's an obvious fact that the Drill Sergeant is wearing dark green khaki slacks (the necessary ingredient for Khaki Fever) tucked into his boots, and a heavy, rainproof jacket that's also lined in khaki fleece.

He hoists the main pipe up onto his khaki-clad leg, and like a seasoned professional, he begins to saw off the banged up end of it. It seems pretty simple at first, but the more I watch him, the more I am becoming enchanted by his barbaric grunts and orders as he hacks and saws through the thick plastic.

Once complete, he reaches for a large black gasket, one that he had commanded another ranger to find in the reeds when we arrived. That ranger had fumbled desperately wanting to please the Drill Sergeant. When he found it, he jumped up and down, eagerly presenting it to the Drill Sergeant, who merely snatched it out of his hand in disgust. I have the perfect seat to watch him from the truck. What a sight.

Before he attaches the gasket, he has to remove the old pipe that is stuck inside the gasket. He pries at it with a pair of pliers, ripping apart the pipe with brute strength. Sweat is forming on his brow and flies begin to dive-bomb his face to taste his salty sweat. Anyone else would be swatting at their distraction, but he is unaffected by them. He looks up at the truck and beckons me over with one annoyed wave of his arm.

I blindly obey him and scramble over the slippery bank in my tennis shoes. Arriving at his side, I am bamboozled by his authoritative air of confidence. He takes off his coat and passes it to me. I giggle out loud as I accept it. The young rangers look at me questioningly. Even I don't know why I just giggled. I hold on to it tightly, feeling the softness of the khaki fleece as he grunts out reprimands at his co-workers.

He attaches the pipe back to the pump and signals to the other ranger to power it up. It sputters and pops, and then with a deafening rumble, it spits a puff of smoke into the air and hums into its routine pumping cycle. I choke on the scent of petrol and wave the smoke out of my face. As a last resort, I cover my face with his coat. The khaki fleece brushes against my cheek, and his scent overpowers my senses. I feel a slight flutter in my stomach, and that's when it hits me . . . I've got The Fever.

Ack! I drop his coat in utter disgust, trying to escape his scent and the softness of his coat that, only moments ago, covered those bulging, solid muscles. I must regard him for what he really is, a Neanderthal.

However, never before have a pair of black rubber boots looked so sexy. There's nothing sexy about black rubber boots— what the hell am I thinking? This is the fever, that wretched, hideous, Khaki Fever.

My hormones are multiplying by the second in this battle of passion, turning me into a raging rhinoceros myself. In any moment, my actions will make thrashing a pump look like a mere inconvenience. He possesses some type of potency, vigor, and prowess over me beyond my control. Before now, I would have thrown myself at the lions before I threw myself at him.

I will not succumb to this fever, I can't allow myself. I must remember all of his annoying traits; his aloofness, his indecipherable accent, and his words that aren't really words that litter almost every sentence he utters. And I can't forget about his incessant smoking habit, his inability to carry out a conversation, his simplicity . . . that innocent simplicity that is so sweet. *Stop it!* There is nothing innocent about it, it's hillbillyish. He is a hillbilly Neanderthal, plain and simple. Yet, there's something incredibly sexy about that rugged hillbillyness, something I would like to . . . pleh! *Spit out those treacherous thoughts, you imbecile!*

If these feelings don't dissipate in a hurry, I will be forced to throw myself into the watering hole. His momentary blips of reasoning cannot erase the fact that he is my nemesis. At least that is what I have to convince myself of. He is my nemesis, my hero . . . no, my nemesis. My nemenistic hero, or is he my heroic nemesis? There is nothing attractive about him. So what if he has strong legs and strong arms and beautiful brown curls that dangle around the

back of his neck, and the greenest emerald eyes that I . . . aaaahhhhhh
. . . this is a disaster.

I must keep my wits about me; must not lose it now. Only a couple of days to go, I can fight this fever. I have survived being pursued by a lion, attacked by elephants, being stuck in a mud pit with a crocodile, and the terror of sleeping in a tent. I can protect myself from this. This is immaterial compared to everything else. Actually, it's not. Matters of the heart are more dangerous and unpredictable than anything else. Shit.

Not now, not when I'm so close to the end. The end . . . the shark dive is the finale to this adventure, the last fear I have to conquer, and it's only a couple of days away. I need to focus on that, instead. But, I can't. I can't stop looking at him. I will pierce these eyes out if I have to—these obsessed eyes that can't look away. He is going to notice me gawking at him. He will know he has defeated me, beaten me, and weakened me.

The Drill Sergeant looks over at me. Dear God, look relaxed, aloof, and stop smiling, dammit.

"You all right?" he asks.

"Yes. Fine." I try to sound as calm as possible.

"Hmmm, all right then. Let's take lunch. I've got the biggest challenge yet for you this afternoon."

If only he knew how challenging it is to stand before him right now without doing something unsightly.

No need to eat lunch today. A cold shower is far more important than eating. This is the best thing to do when one notices the first signs of a fever coming on, and for best results, follow this with yet another cold shower.

26

Peace Treaty

When the Drill Sergeant arrives, I'm still shivering from the anti-fever cold-water therapy. I had contemplated feigning illness and being unable to work this afternoon, but didn't want to throw away my final day.

"I've got to go to one of the neighboring farms," he says.

"For what?"

"Shoot a cow. She won't stand up."

"Another one?"

"Yep. Do you want to come or not?"

"Not really. What can I do instead?"

"Well, there is one job you can do," he pauses. "It's not very exciting, but no one else wants to do it."

"What is it?"

"You can clean up the garden."

"There's a garden here?"

"Yes, it's in the tent camp. You haven't noticed it?"

How could I not have seen a garden in my very own tiny plot?

The Drill Sergeant walks me to a triangle of land on the corner of the tent camp, beside the elephant stable. An electrical fence surrounds a desolate patch of dry, cracked earth, littered with puddles and stringy dying plants that were randomly placed in no particular order. I'm tempted to laugh. "This is a garden?"

"Yup, there are seeds in the stable if you feel inclined to plant something. Enjoy your day," he says, trudging off.

"Wait, what is this garden for? Does anything actually grow here?"

The Drill Sergeant returns, looking a little irritated, but gives me the long and short of this failed project. "The garden was created for teaching purposes, sustainable living. All the food generated was to be donated to a local village. But nothing will grow here, just a few tomato plants."

"Those are tomato plants? Why won't anything grow here? Porcupines?"

"No. The porcupines don't even want this garden."

"So what happened to it then?"

"It failed for many reasons; lack of resources to build and sustain a garden, drought, and the shitty soil conditions, of course."

The garden project had been passed around the reserve because tending to a garden isn't high on most testosterone-driven rangers' priority lists. It doesn't quite stack up there with handling lions, crocodiles, and elephants. Therefore, the project was put on the back burner for a rainy day, something that has seldom happened in the last century. The Drill Sergeant leaves as fast as he can, obviously no different than the other rangers who have no interest in this project.

The only tools to use will be the heavy, rusty, prehistoric tools in the stable. I've heard of planting a garden in harsh conditions before, but even the moon could sustain more life than this desolate plot.

The elephants aren't in the stable, so there's no risk of Kittibon spitting water or hurling branches at me. Harrison—the human, not the truck—is watching a soccer match in his quarters. Even over the buzz of the vuvuzelas (the terrible horns invented for sports fans to blow into during sporting events), I can hear his bad habit through the thin walls.

The stable looks like a pigsty. Tools are scattered everywhere, the floor is covered in wood shavings, and the wheelbarrow is still full of dung. The wheelbarrow is still full of dung . . . It hits me, just like it hit me across the face on so many cold mornings. Except this time it's not whipped at me from the trunk of a domineering female elephant. Ellie dung. Ellie dung is the solution to this garden! I can't believe there is a deeper meaning to all that dung I've had to endure. Kittibon can make a contribution around here after all.

The dung will hold water, be easy to plant in, and act as fertilizer. There's an endless supply of crap here. These giants make mountains of it daily. Bless the over-worked bowels of Kittibon, they will sustain life after all!

Getting the wheelbarrow into the garden space is difficult. The Drill Sergeant neglected to tell me how to turn off the electricity running through the fence. The technique employed is to tip the wheelbarrow back so the front wheel clears the lower wire, and then going through the other side myself and pulling it through. The slightest wrong movement will result in being zapped by a few thousand volts.

Load after load after load of dung is carted in from the nearby mountain of dung storage. Then each ball is whacked and flattened into patties with the heavy rusty shovel. My arms, back, and legs are on the brink of exhaustion—this is like no gardening I have ever done before—but this garden has a much higher purpose than any other.

After many hours and countless wheelbarrow loads, the garden is coming together in the form of a deep plot of luscious-looking dung.

Just as I dump the last load of dung, I sense someone behind me. Slowly turning around, her monstrous presence shadows me.

Kittibon reaches her long trunk over the wire fence, inhaling only inches away from my head. I drop to the ground, to get just out of her reach. Under me is the pile of green tomato plants I pulled out earlier. She stretches her trunk long, getting even closer. I reach beside me and pluck a sickly-looking green tomato from the ground and offer it to the beast. She sucks it right out of my fingers, curls her trunk up in one snap, and lobs the tomato into her mouth.

Before I can move, her trunk is in my face again. I humbly offer her another tomato, and she sucks it up with even more force, repeating the process again. This time I pick up a tomato and lob it over the fence, just beside her, which gives me enough time to get on my feet and out of her reach. Selati has now joined her at the fence. There are branches and stones on the ground all around them. Is there going to be another battle?

Kittibon and Selati both raise their trunks high above their heads and open their huge, gaping mouths, revealing mouthfuls of flat, white teeth. I toss a tomato into Kitty's mouth. Then I toss one to Selati, where it hits the target, but before he can close his mouth on it, Kittibon reaches her trunk inside his mouth and steals it.

The green tomatoes are a treat. Kittibon bats her long lashes at me. She can be so charming when she chooses to be. The Drill Sergeant was right, she is a typical female. It's going to take more than eyelashes to get more tomatoes.

"Shake!"

Each time I said this to Kitty in the past, she answered me with a trunk full of dung to my face, defying any outside authority. Today she won't shake either; instead she only opens her mouth wider.

"Shake." I say it louder this time in a deep voice.

She doesn't move, either. This is a monumental standoff, but it is nothing more than a mind game — a war of wits.

"Shake!" I yell it this time in an even deeper voice, and as I yell it, I take one step towards her.

There is a long pause as we square off with each other. Last time we did this, she broke Harrison's face when she whipped a rock at me. But not this time. I can't believe it. She is actually shaking her head from side to side. It's slow and more of a half-effort, but she does it. I toss a handful of tomatoes into her mouth and then into Selati's. This small act of sharing tomatoes signifies a colossal moment in international elephant relations.

After the final tomato is tossed to Kittibon, she strolls away without any unprovoked assaults. It's official; a peace treaty has been reached.

With peace in place, it's time to plant some seeds in this fertile plot of poop. There are two packages of peas and two packages of lettuce. It's not much, but it is a starting point.

Using a discarded ellie branch, I make rows of two-inch-deep trenches. The ellie branches are then used as rustic markers at the end of each row. It looks primitive, but it fits in just fine here.

Big and round, the pea seeds are easy to plant. The lettuce seeds, on the other hand, are tiny and tedious to plant; one tiny seed in, cover it, and move on. Another tiny seed in, cover it, and move on.

Out of the monotony, a voice is heard:

"You're not fearless." The voice comes from deep within. It is Fear himself.

"Yes I am."

"No, you're not. You need me."

"I don't need you."

"You need me to protect you."

"Protect me from what?"

"From being alone. Without me, you are all alone. All those nights in your tent I distracted you. I saved you."

"I didn't need you. I've been sleeping in my tent, without you, no problem. You made me look like a fool."

"Without me, you would have to look at yourself, and that is more terrifying than anything I have shown you."

"This is crazy. I don't know what you're talking about."

"You need me to protect you."

"From what?"

"From what is growing inside of you. It chips away at your spirit and cripples you. Without me to protect you from seeing it, it would engulf you from within and destroy you."

"What is *it*?"

Fear goes silent.

There is nothing crippling me. I am stronger than ever. I'm not running anymore. I've come to terms with Death and accepted it. What can be more devastating than loss?

~~~

When I open my mother's bedroom door, her scent overtakes my senses and fills the room as though she is there. Her bedroom had remained untouched since the night we went to the hospital. Her old slippers with the paisley print still sit on the floor beside her bed, waiting for feet to slide into them. The covers are pulled back. On her bedside table a dime store paperback is dog-eared just a few pages in. Beside it sits a glass of water, half empty on a coaster, protecting the teak wood underneath. My father's smiling portrait faces her pillow.

I set the ivory-colored porcelain urn on the dresser, beside my father's. I open the white "Patient's Belongings" plastic bag and begin pulling the Christmas cards out, one by one. I set them up around her urn, filling the dresser.

A cedar chest sits at the end of her bed. On it, her suitcase is set open. She had packed her holiday clothes for our beach holiday that never came to pass. I gently lower the flap of the suitcase.

I walk over to the mirrored closet door and slide it open. Rolls of wrapping paper, scissors, tape, and a bag of Christmas bows lie on the floor. My gift lies beside them, still unwrapped.

Thirty years. Thirty years this had been my family's home. Now it is nearly empty, filled with memories, and the only memories I can bring to mind are the most recent ones. The painful ones that haunt me every time I allow my mind to wander — particularly in that moment right before falling asleep. The memories, so fresh and disturbing, they jolt me upright in bed. It was not Death or Fear I had been running from all this time.

27

A Demon is Exposed

The Drill Sergeant calls over the garden fence. "Are you ready for your biggest challenge yet?"

I had forgotten all about him and the final challenge he keeps threatening me with. "Sure."

"Then get in and buckle up, it's gonna be a bumpy ride!" He is smiling from ear to ear.

Buckle up? I've forgotten what it even feels like to wear a seatbelt. Such a luxury has long since been forgotten.

If it is another harrowing escape from the lion camp, then I am ready for it. If it is another croc pit confrontation, then bring it on. And if it is building another road with a raging hormonal rhinoceros, then what the heck, why not? And Kittibon? We're old friends now.

Moments later we arrive at the maintenance shack.

The Drill Sergeant parks in front of the maintenance shed. "Come along," he says, motioning me to follow him.

I follow him around the back to the slaughterhouse where I first saw the cow's carcass. As we approach, the stagnant reek emanating from within thickens the air into a putrid pit of grotesqueness. My knees go weak.

Just as before, the reek worsens the closer we get, making my stomach churn. I cover my nose with my bandana to lessen the effects of the smell, but that doesn't stop it from tempting my stomach contents to resurface. The Drill Sergeant goes in first.

"Why are we here?" I finally ask.

"This is your final challenge, Melissa," he says, pulling back the heavy plastic curtain.

Suspended from a cold steel hook is the body of the hartebeest. Plunk. My heart hits the bottom of my stomach.

"Last chance to prepare a carcass. The silly old hartebeest, remember her?" he laughs.

Of course I remember her. I will never forget her.

"Are you ready?" he asks.

I can't take my eyes off her. Her own eyes are still wide open. I can't possibly butcher her. She looks so delicate and sad.

Clink, clink, clink. The Drill Sergeant taps a long steel knife against the wire cable suspended above.

"Yes? No? I didn't think so." He laughs, "Wait outside, you big chicken." He releases the curtain, closing it.

From behind the curtain, there's a loud tearing noise, as he slices open her throat, ripping open the jugular vein. Gush. Fluid splashes onto the concrete. A thick river of blood edges out from under the curtain. A consistent drip echoes as her vessels empty.

I close my eyes and try to block the noise.

"You're not a chicken; you're a coward. You stripped away her last shred of hope. You told her to die, and then you left her to die alone."

Who the hell is this monster?

"You got mad at your siblings for leaving, but you're worse than they are. She relied on you. You were what she was clinging on to, and you abandoned her."

"I didn't abandon her. I couldn't stand the noise. She was drowning in her own lungs. There was nothing I could do for her."

"If you were dying, she would have never left your side."

"Who are you? Why are you saying these terrible things?"

"I am your conscience. Your guilty conscience, the one you have been trying to ignore. Fear can't silence me anymore. You know what you did."

"It's true. I left the room. When my own mother was dying, I left the room. She was drowning. They put an oxygen mask over her face and had it turned up full blast. It was loud, but I could still hear her gurgling. That sound, that horrible sound, she was suffering. I was helpless. There was nothing I could do."

"You could have stayed with her instead of leaving her to die alone."

"I couldn't stay. I couldn't take it anymore."

"Your mother suffered in her final hours. She was fighting for breath, fighting for her life, drowning within herself. She was a strong woman, and she did not give up easily. The battle lasted for hours. She was all alone and she knew it. You told her to go. You told her to die."

"I knew when I came back and she was dead that I should have never left. She was there in the room, but I couldn't look at her. I was too ashamed. I knew she would be disappointed in me. She always knew when I was there, and when I wasn't there, she always waited for me to come back. She wouldn't sleep unless I was there. I let her down. 'I abandoned her when she needed me most. You're right. I am a coward."

28

A Demon is Slaughtered

"I told you that you needed me." Fear has returned and is trying to take control away from me.

"I don't need you."

"Yes you do. Guilt is what I was protecting you from. There is nothing crueler than Guilt."

"It's true, you distracted me and, like an alcoholic, I drank in your distractions, addicted to the numb feeling they left me with. But I don't need you anymore."

I pulled back the curtain. "Give me the knife." My voice is as cold as steel. The Drill Sergeant jumps slightly.

"What?"

"Give me the knife." I repeat.

"You don't have to do this, I was only teasing you."

"It's all right. I want to do it. Tell me what to do."

Fear speaks up. "Don't do this."

"I'm letting you go, I don't need you anymore, Fear."

"Without me you're dead."

"Without you, I'm alive."

"I filled the void when your mother died."

"I was afraid to be alone, but I'm not afraid anymore."

"Without me you will be engulfed by guilt and live a painful life."

"I was helpless. Exhausted. I had been beaten down to nothing. I did everything I could with what I had at the time. I have nothing to feel guilty about."

"You're a coward."

"I am not a coward."

"Start here," the Drill Sergeant points.

I drove the dagger deep into the hartebeest's rear hip.

"Keep pushing until you hit bone," the Drill Sergeant says from behind me.

I try to drive the knife in further, but the flesh is raw and tough. I push hard with all my strength. "Aaaahhhhhhhhhhhhhh," I scream as I drive the knife in further, using my arms, my legs, and every other muscle in my body—slaughtering everything that dead hartebeest represents: Fear, Shame, Grief and Guilt.

The knife hits bone with a blood-curdling screech. Then the knife seems to take on a life of its own, slicing and chopping its way through tendons and muscle, *schlik, slosh, schlik.* I feel through the moves, trying not to look as the leg becomes loose, exposing the mutilated insides.

Each time the knife makes contact with bone, it makes a grating noise. The knife catches, and I rip it harder. Blood sprays onto my jeans and shoes, staining them with dark red splotches.

Finally, the hip loosens its grip on the leg, and it swings unnaturally back and forth. I hold onto it tightly with one gloved hand to keep it in place. As the tendons are cut away, I release my grip on her leg, and the final motions of my knife become redundant as the weight of the leg pulls it from the body. Thud. It hits the floor, landing in a puddle of blood. The Drill Sergeant picks up the long leg and tosses it into a crate.

Stepping around to the other side, I hold the handle of the knife tightly with two hands and drive it in with force. As the knife pierces her hide, a confetti of blood sprays over the front of me, but this doesn't stop me, or even slow me down. Now I am used to the bloodshed, each tear of flesh eradicates Fear, silencing him for good. The front legs are easier to amputate and weigh less than half of her hind legs. A wave of relief washes over me when the last leg hits the ground.

"This is how you remove the hide," says the Drill Sergeant as he moves his arms through the air.

I make a long incision and begin to pluck away at her red fur coat, going deeper within.

With Fear hacked away, the gory battle with Guilt is now well underway. I chop away at him, stabbing him, ripping him apart. He fights back, but I am not backing down. I hadn't realized how I had lost control when I thought I was gaining it. I hadn't realized how I had let Guilt consume me. Mum understands why I had to let her go. I did the best I could. I did the best I could. I did the best I could.

I jab and stab, and am unstoppable until the entire hide is gone, leaving behind marbled flesh. The butchering continues. I carve large sheaths of meat from her sides and chest; it's a long and bloody process. I cry tears of release, releasing the guilt that was born the day my mother died and that I had nurtured until it grew into a festering monster.

When I am finished there is no meat left on the carcass, only her head, spine, ribs and organs remain intact. I place the bloody knife into the Drill Sergeant's hand.

I am covered in blood from head to toe. It was gruesome, but the circle is finally closing.

29

Finding Inyanga, Finding Freedom

"Jesus," the Drill Sergeant finally says. "Are you all right?"

I nod. "I'm all right." My voice is shaking, but the tears have stopped. Everything is brighter, lighter.

"You didn't have to do all that." He's either impressed or thinks I've finally snapped.

"I may have gotten a little carried away."

"You sure you're all right?" The Drill Sergeant doesn't quite recognize this chick from the city anymore.

"Yeah, I'm good. Really good." A long, deep sigh escapes from the bottom of my lungs. The hardest thing I ever did was let my mum go. I held on to her so tightly in those last few weeks. Day after day I lay in that bed with her, squeezing her hand, forcing the life to stay in her. I was terrified to let go. I was afraid of the emptiness that would follow. Her health declined, and my guilt grew.

Our roles began to blur in those last few weeks. She relied on me heavily. I relied on her, too, but didn't let her see the magnitude of my reliance. But she felt it, and that's why she held on, for me. She really believed she was going to go home. I allowed her to believe that, I encouraged it. I wanted to protect her from the truth, and anyone who told her otherwise was cut-down by me. She was afraid when I wasn't there. I wanted to protect her as she had always done for me. She gave me life, but I couldn't save hers.

In the time since she passed, I buried my grief in one distraction after another—some bad, some good—anything not to face the reality that my mum was gone forever. But left unchecked, my grief turned to guilt and there is no demon viler than guilt. Had I allowed myself to grieve before, my mother's death wouldn't have given birth to this guilt that has been left to grow and fester. Being exposed to death and dying again has allowed me to go through the process. That hartebeest was more than just a hartebeest. Her death allowed me to openly grieve, and she allowed me to watch death consume and ultimately take her as it did to my mother.

I wept for that hartebeest the way I should have allowed myself to when my mother died. That hartebeest released within me the grief I had been carrying since my mum died. When my grief came to the surface, so did guilt, guilt that had no right to be there in the first place, I see that now. I did the best I could. I did everything I could. And that was enough, it was enough. The hartebeest's death has given my life back to me.

And as the Drill Instructor keeps drilling into my head, the gift of her meat will provide life to the cheetahs.

The Drill Sergeant appears with a large crate of the meat I just butchered. We'll go to the cheetah camp first, then head out onto the reserve to find Inyanga. She is due for a calcium supplement that we'll inject into the meat.

When we arrive at the cheetah camp, there's a small crowd of tourists watching them from just outside of the fence. The Drill Sergeant gives them a nonchalant nod as we each carry one side of the meat crate inside. Inside the enclosure is another enclosure, where one adolescent cheetah has escaped into the outer compound. He begins to approach us as soon as we go in. I instinctively crouch down, as one would do with a domestic cat.

"Get up!" roars the Drill Sergeant.

"Why?" I say, embarrassed, as he yanks me up by my shoulder.

"You know not to crouch down in front of a cheetah," he snarls, "He'll claw your throat out."

There are loud gasps from the audience of tourists. The cameras have stopped. Their eyes only are on me now, eyes that seem to say, "What were you thinking?"

The Drill Sergeant didn't have to make me look like an idiot in front of all these strangers. The cheetahs pace back and forth, fixated on the meat, hissing and growling. I purposely make quick turns to try and outrun the cheetah, but they can sense my next move before I even take it. The crowd loves the show I'm putting on, and I feel like I have regained my standing as a ranger, in their eyes, at least. The only one not impressed is the Drill Sergeant.

I toss the first piece of meat over the high fence to a young male who is perched back on his hind legs, ready to spring. While it is still high in the air, he jumps up and snatches it, shaking it violently back and forth, shredding the meat. The next cheetah charges the fence and even gets a shock, but he doesn't back down, he snarls and hisses, only irritated by the shock. I throw the meat over to him quickly before he shocks himself again.

The feeding frenzy, and show, is over. We leave the enclosure, and I bow to the small crowd. I'm just about to say something clever when the Drill Sergeant interrupts me. "This is our current volunteer. She is learning the workings of a game reserve and, as you can see, even after spending every day with wildlife, it's still easy to make enormous mistakes."

My face grows hot with embarrassment, and it takes everything in me not to kick his ass in front of the tourists. After everything we've been through, how dare he mock me like that?

"Yes, I see that, mmhmm," a tourist observes.

Quickly leaving the enclosure behind, I swing around as soon as we are out of earshot. "What the hell was that?"

The Drill Sergeant slides into the truck, shaking his head.

I am seething. "You made me look stupid!"

"You were being stupid," he said, his voice rising. "You know you can't let your guard down for a second with wildlife, especially cats. You could have lost your hand in there. Tourists see you do that, and what happens? They follow your lead. When we make stupid mistakes it's the animals that suffer. They get blamed for our stupidity when they do what comes naturally to them."

"Well you didn't have to embarrass me!"

"I merely stated the truth. This is not a petting zoo, nor is it a circus. You were giving those tourists the wrong impression about wildlife. They don't have the one-on-one training you've had."

What he says is true, but his delivery stinks. I'm more embarrassed at making such stupid mistakes this far in than I am angry with him. But there's no time to dwell on it. I have to lick my wounds and get moving, since the sun will be setting soon, and there's still much to do.

We head out on the reserve to find Inyanga. The roaming cheetahs wear electric collars, and we have antenna to track them, but that doesn't guarantee they'll be found quickly. We have spent many a day tracking in the past only to come up with nothing.

We arrive at the spot where the cheetahs were seen earlier this morning. The Drill Sergeant climbs up onto Harrison's hood, holding the large tracking antenna in one hand and the radio in the other, turning in circles trying to pick up a signal, but no luck. He jumps down onto the ground and tries again, but there's only static on the radio, no beeps. He huffs and throws the antenna into the back of the truck.

Tracking a cheetah is the final task at the reserve, an easy send off after three weeks of physically and mentally grueling work. I use to think the crappiest experience was cleaning out the elephant stables every day, but over time that job proved beneficial in clearing out my own crap. Had it not been for those monstrous balls of dung and the Drill Sergeant leaving me to do the work alone, it could have taken me a lifetime to uncover and eliminate my demons.

The crappy chore had caused an internal shakedown, a fundamental butt-kicking of old habits. For most of my thinking life, my mind had the habit of filling itself with non-serving thoughts and beliefs. Bits of random useless data were able to run freely, completely occupying my consciousness, and my autopilot brain just took them as reality, never questioning, never blocking, just blindly accepting them as is. But in the last few weeks, every morning, at the crack of dawn, I was forced to spend time one-on-one with my thoughts, catching and deciphering this useless data. It was like an internal fridge clean, and I found myself picking up items and thinking, *What the hell am I holding on to that for?*

The human mind is much bigger than a fridge, or elephant stable, for that matter. It is easy to keep stuffing it with stinky, smelly, useless beliefs that don't leave any space for anything of real value, like compassion, openness, courage, understanding, and the highly sought after delicacies of acceptance and forgiveness of oneself.

I probably never would have done this mental cleanup had I not come to volunteer in Africa. The stable cleaning required all my physical attention, but none of my cognitive skills. All I had to do was shovel and toss. I couldn't distract myself with the phone, TV, email, traffic, or even the ultimate mind-numbing distraction of the 20th Century: Spider Solitaire. My mind was left completely undistracted from its own senseless ramblings, and as much as I tried to avoid it, it was eventually forced to confront itself, for there *was* nothing else.

During this resistance, things that had previously held a permanent position in my consciousness (like the mysterious contents of the Chinese take-out box) were slowly eradicated, one heavy shovel load at a time. And I do mean heavy.

One of the first to go was the fixation of my physical appearance, particularly my butt, and whether it was expanding in all the wrong directions. I literally kicked that obsession in the butt and out of my mind for good. If it is expanding, so what; it will give me something softer to land on the next time I hit a bump in the road. If people want to stare at it, point and laugh—which I don't think has ever actually happened—then let them.

The precious real estate in my mind can no longer be wasted housing a ghetto of self-deprecating thoughts. Those thoughts have been evicted, and that space is now on the market, but only for seriously committed thoughts, thoughts that will enhance the neighborhood, not pollute it.

Other beliefs were hard to remove. I questioned if they were really meant to go, or if I should hold on to them just in case I needed them one day—like the expired bottles of rare condiments that take up all the door shelf space but serve no logical purpose. These beliefs were rooted deeply in a place that was kept dark, making them hard to find, and even harder to excavate. These beliefs kept me in my comfort zone of safe and predictable routines, and even more predictable outcomes. They had to go. Those stubborn beliefs were the ones that, once gone, left me feeling lighter and relieved to have that valuable space back for something useful like all the good times I had with my family, or these new memories of Africa, where no outcome is predictable and I'm so far away from the boundaries of my comfort zone that I can't even see it with a telescope.

Some were old skeletons that had been mummified by complicated clutter, being hoarded only to serve as a reminder of mistakes from the past. It felt awesome to kick the crap out of those skeletons.

Then, there were the cleverly disguised false truths that were so entwined in stubborn habits that it made them nearly impossible to throw out. Those were the ones that required me to roll up my sleeves and give it my all. I use to complain about what I didn't have, thinking I didn't have enough and that I would just be happy if . . . Africa has shown me how rich I am and that "things" don't make me rich.

Then there was the fluff that served no purpose whatsoever other than to feed the false beliefs and fear monsters my mind had spent years creating and housing. Some were there since longer than I can remember, placed there by my earliest influences: parents, siblings, and teachers. The fluff was the easiest of all to remove; in fact, I found myself laughing aloud as I noticed just how ridiculous it was. Like being afraid to swim in a pool alone for fear of being attacked by a shark. Or fear of smiling at a stranger on the street or, heaven forbid, actually complimenting a stranger.

And when everything else had been cleared away, there was just one thing remaining: that mystery Tupperware container hidden deep within, the one that has always been there. The lid tightly sealed, hiding the contents within. Everyone has a mystery Tupperware container. The one we push to the back and block with fancy mustards and olive jars that are rarely used — mere distractions to what's hiding behind.

Having the courage to remove that Tupperware and exposing the revolting contents within — the parasites, the maggots, the vile moving bacteria that have been able to fester for years — are necessary for a complete cleanse. Because once exposed with all its raw ugliness, it can finally be tossed, flushed, and forgotten for good because who in their right mind would put it back in the fridge? A lot of us do — after all it's always just "been there" and the shelf feels lacking without it.

However, once removed, freedom can finally move into that space. Guilt filled the contents of my Tupperware container. The seeds had been planted early, how and by whom I'm not really sure, and it doesn't really matter anyway. Perhaps they were just silly childhood notions that were left to grow out of control. But when my mother died, guilt grew into an overbearing monster that consumed me and sucked me into its void of horror. I was in so deep that I didn't even realize what had happened. I was shell-shocked.

But here in Africa, I gained the courage to open the lid and examine the contents within. Yes, they were ugly, and yes they were brutal, but they weren't real.

"Hey look at that!" I say, pointing to one of the roads we just repaired.

One side of the road has sunk and looks like someone or something has dug up all our carefully lain rocks and strewn them as far away as he could. We get out of the truck to inspect the damage more closely, and that's when the Drill Sergeant sees the evidence that the culprit left behind. The hormonal rhino has left his calling card in the way of two long parallel lines in the dirt; it's his way of marking his territory. First he urinates, and then he drags his legs in it, hence the parallel lines. This gets the smell on his legs and feet, and then he patrols his area, depositing his scent to let everyone else know this is his territory.

A garbled message comes over the radio from another ranger; Inyanga has just been seen in the central thicket, close to where we are. We continue our search on foot, this time tracking her prints in the sand.

"There she is," the Drill Sergeant whispers.

He has the carcass's hind leg swung over his shoulder as he slowly approaches her. She's skulked down and moves towards us quickly, as though we are the prey.

"Let me do it." I whisper.

I take the leg from his hands but the unexpected weight of it pulls it through my gloves, and it drops to the ground. I hoist it up over my shoulder and start walking towards Inyanga, who is moving even faster towards us.

"Take a picture," I say, handing my camera to the Drill Sergeant.

I stop and let the weight of the limb rest on the ground and lean it up against my blood-soaked jeans. I wait. She's coming even faster now, her eyes cutting through me, she is fearless.

"Drop it and back away," the Drill Sergeant orders.

I don't move. I can't move. She captivates me. She is magnificent. I am engulfed by her spell. Will she leap and pounce on me? Will she think my bloody legs and the carcass are one and the same? Will she jump on my throat and take me down? No, she will not do any of those things, for I am in control.

"You're crazy, drop it now!" the Drill Sergeant hisses.

She slows her pace a few yards in front of me. Her lips peel back as she opens her mouth revealing razor sharp fangs. A low, deep growl slowly erupts from her bowels and grows louder with every inch it rises. I lean the bloody leg away from my own so she doesn't try to take them both.

I stand tall, remembering everything the Drill Sergeant had taught me, not making the same mistakes I did earlier. The Drill Sergeant is silent. I can't see him. I have to keep my eyes on her, not giving her a second to catch me off guard.

She moves forward, glaring at me through narrowed eyes. I hold her eyes and stretch each and every one of my vertebrae to its limits, making myself as tall as possible.

With one fast strike, she snatches the leg from my hand. She backs away, eyes still on mine her powerful jaws holding the heavy leg up high in the air. I back away slowly as well, keeping my eyes on her. She disappears into the thicket, her camouflage coat instantly invisible.

"That was awesome!" I shout, and put up a high five for the Drill Sergeant, which he ignores.

"You're crazy. That was reckless and dangerous." But underneath his act of anger, the Drill Sergeant is trying not to smile with pride for his student.

We climb back into Harrison to make the final journey back to my tent camp, mainly in silence. It isn't until we arrive that the Drill Sergeant finally speaks. "It's your last night. Do you want to watch a game with me?"

This is it. I can surrender and allow, or I can go and hide in my tent alone. "Yes, I do want to."

30
Hope

South Africa scored many times the previous night, but they never won the game. The Drill Sergeant and I, however, have a new camaraderie. This unlikely mutual respect has grown from an original repulsion to stronger than fire and water. Just like my neighbors, the enigma known as Bonty and Wildebeest, the Drill Sergeant and I have come to a mutual respect for each other's disparities.

Instead of trying to kill each other, Bonty and Wildebeest live here together in peace. I had spent so many days observing them, trying to figure out why they hadn't tried to kill each other. Surely, these habitual murderers would want to kill an outsider, someone who wasn't of their own kind. But they don't and, instead, they live together in peace.

On the outside, they have nothing in common, but when I look more closely, I see that underneath, below their awkward or cute exteriors, they are very much the same. They are two strangers that suffer from the same afflictions of loneliness and being misunderstood.

Once outcast from society, another similarity has become apparent, one that can only be seen when in solitary confinement. Their camp is wide open and there aren't too many trees to hide behind or brush to get lost in, so they are both out on display, unable to hide from one another.

Once everything else is stripped away, they realize that they just have each other. That kinship is what keeps these two ruffians from killing each other, and from dying of loneliness.

Therefore, this enigma is no longer an enigma, it is a partnership between opposing forces, and one that offers hope— hope that reaches far beyond the borders of this tiny microcosm of society. Despite what horrors life throws at us, and the challenges that make us question our own faith, hope is what keeps us moving forward, even in the darkness. And Hope is what the Wildebeest's name shall be from this day forward.

31

Super Predators

I recognize a familiar face on the bus to Mosselbaii this morning. It is Rastaman. I take a seat beside him. The only word I had ever heard him say is "crocodile" and that was during the rescue effort. Since then, he hasn't uttered another word, until now.

"Do you know what Rasta means?" he asks in a scratchy, deep voice.

"No."

He takes my journal from my hands and removes a pencil from deep within his dreadlocks. Turning to a clean sheet he writes the word *Seharite*.

"What does that mean?"

"It means sister. You are my sister. We are all sisters and brothers. We are all love. That is the meaning of Rasta. And there is only one love, one love for everybody and everything. People look at me like I'm just a longhaired ganja smoker; I am not. I love everyone. I am peaceful. I respect all people, animals, and things. I am full of love, peace, and harmony. If people looked past my hair and, instead, looked into my heart and soul, then they would see a good man, a man that loves all his brothers and sisters. They would only see love." He is nearly pleading as he says the words without looking at me.

I feel his urgency, his strong desire to put an end to prejudice so it can no longer shadow his own personal truth. His passion about how the world convicts him without knowing him is torturing his spirit. My shark phobia seems insignificant compared to what torments Rastaman.

"I am your sister, Rastaman."

"Yah," he breathes, now gazing out the window.

My acceptance is not enough to release him from the chains of prejudice that bind him.

The drive passes quickly as my head swirls with questions demanding solutions. By the time we reach Mosselbaii, I realize that while I am certainly not the end, I am the beginning. It's not up to "somebody out there" or "some non-profit organization" to change things. I can do something and my time to do it is now, however infinitesimal that it may be. It's a start.

"Good bye Rastaman. I hope I'll see you again, you are a good man, brother." My eyes meet his, and in that nanosecond, I really *see* him. We are just the same, and need the same things. The things that I have found after my own anguishing experience, he will one day find, too.

Rastaman half smiles and nods as I back out of the seat and exit the bus.

My own reality begins to set in as I step onto the pavement. I find the office of the shark dive excursion within a few minutes; one can't miss the huge sign out front that screams, "Great White Shark."

The office is in the middle of town, not on the beach, or in the harbor, making it less intimidating as it gives the illusion of being safe, solid, and dry. Had it been within eyeshot of the ocean, I likely would not find myself inside here now.

I open the door and step forward. There is a lady behind the counter who instantly greets me with a warm smile. "Welcome, come on in!"

There are three couples inside, seated at small café tables. They are busy watching a soccer match on a television screen that is mounted up high on the wall.

I am the only single person here. I move forward to the counter, where a waiver is placed in front of me. "Please sign here," she says, with a hip-width smile that bears striking resemblance to Mama Magda's.

I sign the waiver quickly and slide it back across the desk before hesitation sets in and I change my mind.

"Please, help yourself to breakfast," she says, pointing towards the back corner.

There, laid out across a six-foot table, is the most beautiful spread of food I have seen in weeks. There are cascading mountains of sweet and savory treats of flaky croissants, rolled pastries with jam filling, crescent rolls, deep-fried crepes, doughnuts, and what is this chocolately-looking creation hiding underneath a wrapper? The label says double chocolate muffin with a gooey chocolate center. This is no mere muffin . . . this is a piece of lava cake disguised as a muffin! I have died and gone to heaven.

"Don't eat if you get seasick. You don't want to be hanging your head overboard out there," the nice lady calls over my shoulder.

I do get seasick, but I don't care. If I'm going to get eaten by a shark today then I am going out with a stomach full of chocolate.

I try to make eye contact with someone, hoping to start a conversation, but no one is biting. They don't look too excited to be here, either. Since I don't have anyone to talk to, because I am the only single person here, I may as well just write in my journal. *My fellow shark divers are unfriendly . . .* Wait, I shouldn't write that. What if these strangers have to search through my journal later, looking for an emergency contact number? The waiver I signed didn't even ask for one. I must choose my words carefully, just in case these are the final words I leave behind.

I should write something profound, something insightful, a lasting legacy, something that can be read at my eulogy with pride.

I can't come up with anything. I search the faces of the strangers around me, hoping that something will surface, but I come up with nothing, absolutely nothing. The page is blank.

Another young couple enters the office, the perfect diversion, allowing me to steal a couple more chocolate muffins. Who are these people, anyway? What if someone on the boat is crazy and they boat-jack us? It could happen, carjackings happen every day; it is just a matter of time before one of these shark boats is hijacked. If they're especially horrible terrorists, they'll throw one of us overboard to be eaten alive as a terror tactic. My God, I hope I'm not the one who goes overboard. I haven't been able to write anything! I can't leave a blank page behind. Someone else will have to go. I mean, at least they have someone left behind who can tell their loved ones about their last moments, their final words. My only companion is a journal with a blank page.

One of the crewmates has just come into the office. He must be the skipper, and looks like the star from *Jaws*. This is very reassuring. I think he would save my life, just like he saved so many lives in the movie. Well, in the end he saved them. There had to be a few casualties; after all, it was Hollywood.

The skipper goes into the back office and closes the door. *We were supposed to leave fifteen minutes ago. When are we going?* This waiting is excruciating, and what's making it worse is all I can hear is the buzz of vuvuzelas from the soccer game. It's driving me crazy. The only benefit to this torturous racket is that it hides the sound of the crinkly plastic each time I open one of these damn muffins. Number six is the latest casualty to my jaws; I no longer give a damn about seasickness. It's all a matter of survival now, especially if I'm held at ransom for several days at sea with no food.

I can't stop stuffing chocolate muffins into my mouth. I have become a chocolate shark, devouring each one in a feeding frenzy, no longer caring about hiding the sounds of wrappers . . . and there goes number eight, crap.

I have been waiting for forty-five minutes. There are no more chocolate muffins to distract me from the pending doom. The longer I wait, the harder it is to just sit here. I want to run, run far, far away from this ludicrous idea.

Another crewmember enters the office; this one's stocky and almost as wide as he is tall, all solid muscle. This is reassuring because if the boat goes down in some freak accident, any shark would definitely choose him over me. He looks like a big plump T-bone steak compared to the sinewy sirloin the sharks would take me for. Turns out, he's a volunteer from Alaska. He works in the hospitality industry, but was always fascinated with sharks, so he took a three-month leave of absence to volunteer with this shark research and conservation group.

Why aren't we going? Everyone is calmly watching this stupid soccer game. We are here to go shark diving, not watch TV!!!!! Screw soccer, let's go and get this over with. I can't take it anymore.

Ooooohhh, stocky crew member is looking at his watch. Maybe we're going? Or maybe not, he has reverted back to the television. I will go and scour the buffet table for the next victim. Thankfully, at the very moment I'm about to reach for a jelly roll, the captain announces that it is time to go. Oh shit. My stomach threatens to revolt, while my knees turn to jelly.

It's only a short walk to the marina, straight down a hill lined with brightly painted colonial buildings. At the entrance to the marina is a bright cement block building called the Sea Gypsy Café. It's the last building before the marina and it is taking everything in me not to detour to it in lieu of the boat. I'm petrified. I pass the cafe and continue towards the dock, but I can't really fathom that I am actually going to do this. Logic screams *you're an idiot*, and I know it's true, but my feet continue to shuffle down the marina of their own volition.

The wall around the marina is made of concrete blocks, painted pale blue to look like an ocean, with pictures of smiling seahorses, whales, sharks, swordfish, lobsters, and seals. The friendly painted sea creatures don't make what we're about to do any less unnerving.

Soon, we arrive at a dock and stop at the foot of a cruising boat. It is not as big as I would have liked, and the name on it says, *Shark Warrior*. A friendly crewmember offers me his hand and pulls me aboard.

I take a seat near the front on the lower deck. We're all supposed to gather there for a safety debriefing. There are no lifejackets in sight, and there is no emergency escape dingy either.

The captain will give us the important details of what to do in the case of an emergency, while the crew is busy loading up supplies and big containers of smelly chum. I will take notes of everything he says. At last, I have something to write in my journal.

1. Do not do number two in the toilet, only number one. It doesn't flush properly, and anything you leave in there will be left for the next person.
2. Do not throw up on the deck or inside the cabin. Do it overboard, just make sure a shark doesn't jump out of the water and bite your head off.
3. When we tell you to get in the cage, move quickly, do not hesitate.
4. Do not try and touch a great white shark.
5. Sometimes, a shark will get so close to the cage that he'll put his nose in. Do not freak out; remain calm and, again, do not try and touch him.
6. You will not have a weight belt; you have to hold yourself under water. Only hold on to the upper-inner bar of the cage, do not hold on to the outer bars, as a shark can take off your hand just by grazing it.
7. Keep your feet hooked under the lower-inner bar. Do not allow your legs to leave the cage, for the obvious reason.
8. Fear can make you lose some of your senses, like hearing; we will shout orders to you, so you can hear us.
9. You will not be given an air tank; instead, you will hold your breath underwater.
10. When I shout left, hold your breath, pull yourself down by the bar, and look to the left. If I shout right, look to the right. Try and stay down as long as you can.
11. In the case of an emergency, life jackets are stowed under the benches.

The place we are going is called Seal Island. It often appears on documentaries during *Shark Week* on Discovery Channel. Seal Island, or the mini market, as it's often called, is a stopover point for the sharks on their way west, where their big feeding ground is — or as the locals call it, the supermarket.

As we approach the island, the sound of hundreds of seals sounds like the calls of lost sheep: *baaaaaah, baaaaah, baaah.* The smell, on the other hand, is like a kitty litter box multiplied by a thousand, and it hits everyone at the same time, as we all start choking on the stench of urine. The captain tells us to take five long, deep breaths, and then our noses will be immune to the smell. I'm too afraid to try in case I toss the eight muffins I just ate, and instead cover my face with my shirt.

The crew hands out full-body wetsuits with hoods and masks. I go inside the cabin and pull mine on over my swimsuit, slowly, taking my time. I come back onto the deck and look down at the dark Indian Ocean and the cage that now has been suspended from the side of the boat, there is only one fellow inside, and everyone else is still changing. Damn, I had hoped to be the last one in.

The captain shouts at me. "You there! Come over here and get in the cage!" Does he not realize that getting into that cage is the last thing I want to do? I've been going through the motions, I've made it this far, but I don't actually have to get into the cage, do I?

I do.

A crewmate helps me climb down into the cage. The cool Indian Ocean floods my wetsuit. I hold on tightly to the upper-inner bar while my feet search for the lower bar, finally hooking underneath of it.

The other tourists are taking a long time to get in. Every second feels like an excruciating hour. Hurry up, people! Get in here! Don't you realize how scared I am? I need decoys in here, and yes, I will be the one using you as a human shield should the cage break, so hurry the hell up and get in here, dammit. My bladder is expanding by the second from all the coffee I had earlier.

"May I please get out and use the toilet?" I ask the crewmember. It's like my brain knows if it comes up with a physiological reason for me to get out, I won't have to get back in. After all, I have technically done it, I'm in the bloody cage.

"No, just go in your wetsuit. It'll help attract the sharks," he says. And he's serious!

The guy beside me looks at me with eyes the size of dinner plates and says, "Please don't."

"It's okay, I don't have to go anymore." My bladder is suddenly non-existent, and there is no way even a drop is going to be coming out while at sea.

Once everyone gets into the cage, the lid of the cage is lowered and tied securely in place with heavy rope. We are officially locked in. The captain throws a line overboard, just in front of the cage, with a large chunk of raw meat on it. Everyone holds onto the bar, anticipating the first command.

There is no guarantee we will see great whites, more often than not, tourists leave without one sighting. The captain says this is a rare experience because the sharks are quickly nearing extinction. And it's not just great white sharks that are being annihilated, conservative estimates are 115,000 - 200,000 sharks are hunted every single day around the world. Yes, a day. In just the last fifty years, 90% of the world's sharks have been hunted. And the reason sharks will be extinct in our lifetime? Soup. Shark fin soup is a delicacy in China. Sharks are hunted, finned, then thrown back in the sea to bleed to death. Sharks can't swim without fins. And sharks can't breathe if they're not swimming. The excruciating death by suffocation goes beyond animal cruelty. Eliminating this item from menus will save this species from extinction. It is that simple.

"Get down, to the left!" the captain shouts.

I hold my breath and pull myself down. Gliding just a few inches past us is the most terrifying sight; a dark mass that must be fifteen feet long, much longer than the cage in which we are crouched. As soon as I see it, I scream underwater, a loud, long scream, gulping in water as I do with arms and legs flailing through the bars, outside of the cage. I come up, gasping for air, keeping my eyes on the surface of the water as his fin disappears out of sight.

"Keep your legs in!" the captain screams. "Get down, to the right!"

I pull myself down and search the water for the next super predator that is coming head-on to the cage. I grip the bar as tight as I can to brace for the impact as he smashes the cage right in front of me. His wide open jaws reveal row upon row of teeth—sharp, big teeth that are just two inches from my face. He thrashes his jaws against the cage, ferociously attacking it. I am numb, my body frozen in terror. I dare not move in case my arms or legs flail out again.

My eyes are glued on him. My breath begins to run out, the pressure is building, but I can't move, terrified I'll aggravate him further. This is unbelievable, it's like a dream, yes a dream—not a nightmare, this is a dream come true!

With Fear removed, I see God in these breathtaking creatures, filling me with love, and I have an overwhelming need to protect this species. After a few seconds, he gives up and moves on, and my heart begins to beat again. I pull myself to the surface and gasp for air.

"To the left!" screams the captain.

I gulp down fresh air and pull myself down again just in time to catch the eye of another magnificent creature.

"Down, get down, to the left!" The commands are coming faster and faster. There have to be twenty sharks doing drive-bys, one after the other in quick succession; each one of them just as interested in us as we are in them.

The captain waves the meat right in front of the cage; little bits of it are breaking off and coming into the cage.

"Down, to the right!"

Another shark attacks the front of the cage, his nose pops inside the cage between me and the young man. Our eyes briefly meet, and I see in his what he must see in mine—happiness. A shark's nose is almost on my shoulder. Time stops. My terror melts away, and I feel an immense flood of gratitude and exhilaration overtake me as I lean back, pushing myself away from the bars and the shark. He retreats as quickly as he comes, disappearing into the black sea.

I pull myself up, taking a deep breath, catching the eyes of the other tourists. This time everyone is joyous and friendly; we are now comrades.

"Down, to the right!"

I pull myself under again and again, catching shadows behind me — just out of site. Feeling the displacement of water behind the cage, I'm unable to turn around and see what is right there. Chills race up and down my spine.

At one point a shark even breeches right beside the cage, catching air several feet above. They say this is the only bay in the world where great white sharks breech.

For ninety minutes, we experience the awe and splendor of great white sharks, a rare opportunity to see this endangered species that has survived in the world's oceans for nearly 500 million years, and now are on the brink of extinction at the hands of the biggest super-predator of all: mankind.

I emerge from the cage, floating. I am ecstatic to the core and more alive than I have ever been.

The mood on the boat changes to one of excitement as everyone is chatting and even hugging each other. This group of strangers just had one of the most incredible experiences, and our conquest has bonded us in a way that only a major collective triumph can.

The captain explains that without shark research volunteers, much of the conservation and research work being done to protect sharks would not happen. He goes on to say that if anyone was going to be able to make it happen, it is the volunteers who would be able to make the largest impact in saving this species from extinction. Their experiences would help push through the lobby to make it illegal to hunt sharks around the world.

The captain's father is a leader in having laws passed to protect great white sharks in South Africa. Tourist excursions, like the one today, are what fund shark research by private companies who are passionate to save this species from extinction.

Meeting Jaws one-on-one has changed my perception of him; from terror to one of respect and admiration for his superior strength and survival. I am not only in awe, but am humbled by this highly misunderstood masterpiece of creation. But more than anything else, I am grateful to this super predator for allowing me to finally be free of all fear.

Fear has been replaced with love. I can look at my mother, and when I do, I no longer see illness, suffering, and death. I see a healthy, strong, and amazing woman who has left so much awesomeness behind. I know she was glad I was there and understands why I couldn't be there at the end. She is my mother, she loves me, and that love is what she leaves behind. It is enough. It is more than enough. I miss her. God I miss her, but it's okay, it's finally okay.

The Indian Ocean is now pink with sunset as the boat pulls into the marina. I open my journal and turn to a clean, fresh page. The words that had previously escaped me now flow with great ease — the circle is complete.

32
Farewell

I didn't sleep well at all last night. It wasn't the roar of the lions, the wind flapping the tent walls, the pending shark dive today, that didn't end in gory fashion, after all.

It was because, after three and a half weeks of being here, I wasn't prepared for what was coming this morning, which is the most difficult thing to do yet; leave the reserve. Of course, I knew this day would eventually come, but I hadn't thought too much about the future because I was too busy living in the present and coming to terms with the past.

One can't live in the past, as I learned, because the past is full of inhibitions, fears, and ugly demons. Living in the future wasn't possible, either, because the present was too incredible to ignore. The basics were all I needed or wanted, which was the enjoyment of a simple meal accompanied by a great feeling of accomplishment when a day of physically demanding work and rough conditions closed. It was dangerous working with unpredictable wildlife, and it was harsh when Death made his ugly appearance.

It was easy to live in the moment here because each and every moment gripped me from deep within and forced me to overcome Fear, so I could finally confront and ultimately accept Life. Every moment, I was captivated. Each and every day, I gave sweat and perseverance, trying desperately to even out the balance sheet. But at the end of it all, I received far more than I could ever give. I leave behind a small contribution to the conservation efforts, but take away a lifetime's worth of memories and skills that will see me through anything in the future. They say that to give is to receive, and this has been proven day after day in this small, out-of-the-way place in South Africa, where there's always so much to do and the miracle of giving is always evident.

My initial concerns about coming here seem so silly now when I look back on them.

What if this is financially reckless? I feel richer than I ever have before.

What if I get murdered? I'm still alive.

What if it is ludicrous to cross the globe to volunteer, when I can do it at home? This experience has been so inspiring that it compels me to volunteer more often when I get back home.

Isn't paying to volunteer contradictory? No, in fact, I feel indebted.

What if I get sick? Other than the occasional queasiness, my health is better than ever.

What if I have to go to hospital? It never happened, but if the need arose it was only a short thirty-minute drive.

What if people think I'm being irresponsible? Who gives a damn what people think?

What if I'm eaten by a lion, or worse, half-eaten, and I survive? I narrowly escaped that fate.

Why not wait and do this later in life, when I have loads of leisure time? There are no guarantees of "later in life," or loads of leisure time. The only moment that is guaranteed is the present one.

What about the need to keep up with society's expectations? Society fails to live up to my expectations a lot of the time, so I no longer care what its expectations of me may be.

In conclusion, my concerns were really nothing more than a bunch of hot air — insignificant toots like those of a zebra.

When my mum died, I was angry with God for not listening to my prayers. But God works in mysterious ways. He was listening, and He answered me here, in Africa. When I bowed in service, He knew I was finally ready to hear what He had to teach me. He danced before me in every sunrise and sunset. But that wasn't enough. He sent His whispers on the wind and knocked loudly on my tent walls, and even then, I ran away. He opened the skies, unleashing rivers of rain, but even that couldn't cleanse me of my demons. He polished the window to the universe every time the sun set to remind me I was not alone, but I only saw the brilliance of the sky. He summoned His creatures, one by one — the creatures I naively thought I was there to save — and slowly it began. He led me down a perpetual path of demon crushing, fear busting, and adventure, and somewhere along the way, I finally heard God, and I was able to forgive myself.

Soon, this will all be left behind. I will miss seeing the familiar dark blue coats of these uniformed soldiers who stand thousands of feet high above this valley. I will miss the African sky, the sky that is like no other, with its rainbows and silver-lined clouds, explosive sunrises, and inspiring sunsets. Never once did it fail to impress, and each and every day brought forth an original design even more exhilarating than the last.

The wildlife is, perhaps, the most difficult thing to leave behind. The animals are what inspired me to come here, and despite the gap between species, I have a deep connection with them . . . even Kittibon. I believe she was one of my greatest teachers here. Kittibon means "I have seen." And see, she did. She saw right through me. She saw my skeletons, fears, and guilt, and tried to slap it out of me, until finally I tossed them where they belonged, with the rest of the dung.

Bonty and Hope are also my teachers; they taught me some of the most valuable lessons of all — self-reliance and hope.

The crocodiles reminded me to pay attention to what's lurking just below the surface; otherwise it could bite me in the butt when I least expected it.

What about that funny old hormonal rhinoceros? He reminded me that we all need love, and when we go without, we need to find it within. And just as importantly, we must give love because when we give love, simple love — a smile, a conversation, a genuine wish — even to a stranger, we can change a person's life.

As for the lions, well, the lions reminded me to keep my imagination in check and not let fear rule me. I'm just glad they never did venture beyond their borders.

The cheetah taught me to never back down, no matter how intimidating or ferocious life may seem — always stand strong and stare it down.

About my tent . . . I will even miss sleeping in that tent. That tent gave me more courage than I ever could have mustered up had I continued sleeping in the common area. That tent compelled me to commit to something I, otherwise, never would have done. It proved to me that I can do things I've never done before, and I can do them alone, without someone else shielding me or holding my hand. That tent gave me a lifetime's worth of confidence to step into the darkness of the unknown.

Harrison, with all his flaws, was my chariot, my powerful and faithful chariot that drove me on this journey, proving that surface flaws are not really flaws at all, as they build character. Harrison, with his broken windows, fly-away doors, noisy transmission, rusted-out floor, and lack of any bells and whistles, is and was the perfect vehicle to drive me on this journey. When taken to the limits, when being pursued by lions, he shone — my gleaming chariot is what he always will be.

Then, there is the Drill Sergeant — Gerrit, as he shall be called from now on. Gerrit has pushed me beyond my own limits in every possible way. By leaving me alone, he forced me to be strong. In gaining strength, I was able to slay my demons. By not talking to me, he allowed me to talk with myself. Gerrit, who forced me to do the most difficult and challenging jobs, gave me self-respect. He showed me the freedom of not having to live up to anyone else's expectations, and that my expectations for myself are all that matter.

Gerrit was, perhaps, my greatest teacher of all, in all of his harshness, rudeness, and aloofness, but above all else, his honesty and truism. My fearless leader taught me well how to play with a lion's testicles. My nemesis had become my friend.

~~~

"Are you ready to go?" Gerrit asks.

"Yes, I'm ready."

"Mama Magda wanted me to give you this." In his hands is my teapot.

The little travel teapot, shiny and perfect in every way, has accompanied me on so many journeys, like a faithful companion. "No, tell her she can keep it."

I had cherished that teapot, but it will be more valuable in the Mama Magda's hands than in my own.

The last thing to go in my bag is the gift my mother gave me for Christmas. A pillow she had made of safari design fabric with the Big Five embossed on it. How did my mother know it would be these very animals that I came here to save, and who would end up saving me?

We drive to the bus stop in our usual silence, but today the silence is even deeper than usual. There's an underlying energy of sadness, and it's not just coming from me.

When we arrive at the bus stop it's still dark.

"Do you want me to wait with you?" Gerrit asks.

"No, it's okay. The bus will be here any minute."

"Okay, well, I guess this is it."

"Thank you," My voice continues, "I . . ." Words flow that I have little control over, words that say a lot more than thanks, words that signify so much more than just their meaning, but even these words are unworthy of what I am trying to express.

Gerrit looks me in the eyes for the first time. Before, he always looked past me, something that always annoyed me. Perhaps it wasn't being aloof, perhaps it was a protective mechanism. He doesn't say anything, instead, he pulls me close and hugs me tightly. I nearly melt in his arms, the arms that rescued me more than once, the arms that did nothing while I did the bulk of the physical work on many occasions, and the arms that sometimes even occupied my dreams. His embrace said so much more than my words.

When he finally lets go, he reaches into the back of Harrison and picks up my suitcase. "Should I carry it for you?" he asks.

We both laugh at the offer; after all we have been through together, him carrying my suitcase! Now that's funny. I grab my suitcase and turn away, taking a step towards the bus stop.

I hear him slam Harrison's door, once, twice, three times before it eventually stays closed. The engine turns over, and there's a long *huuuucccck* as he shifts into first.

I begin to walk to the bus stop, momentarily pausing as I strain to hear the words that are whispered from his lips. The words are unmistakable. "Nice butt."

This is followed by one final long whistle.

Author's Note

Grief is an insanely powerful emotion. It is usually paired with guilt, and when combined they can make even the sanest people do insane things. Everybody has their own way of dealing with things, and that's all right. Hindsight is 20/20, but when in the midst of it all, we can be blinded by emotion. Grief is illogical. Grief is excruciatingly painful. With time, grief fades and logic returns but, sadly, sometimes when the anchor of a family is wrenched away, the ones remaining drift apart. But even without an anchor, a strong family unit can better navigate the rough seas ahead. With sails of benevolence and a rudder of empathy, any storm can be conquered.

After my mum died, I filled my life with distraction after distraction to avoid facing grief. Eventually, no distraction would suffice, and I needed more. I needed meaning. I needed purpose. But I didn't know how to find it until one day, when I sat a few feet in front of President Bill Clinton during his Giving tour. Despite feeling like I had nothing in me to give, he inspired me to give it away anyway. I followed my passion for animals and Africa, and threw caution to the wind. That is when the magic happened, a magic that I could have never foreseen in my wildest dreams.

Giving is as simple as smiling at a stranger, donating food, blood, or a few hours to the community. What we can give away at no cost to us is lifesaving to someone else.

The act of giving is what is saving thousands of species from extinction; in fact it is the ONLY thing that is saving these animals from extinction. Volunteers give millions of hours every year to conserve our glorious planet and all the magnificent beings within it. Volunteers are Mother Nature's Ambassadors, but I prefer to just call them angels. My contribution in Africa was tiny; I am not an angel in any shape or form. In fact, the Drill Sergeant would probably have a much more colorful way to describe me, but my experience did lead me to this book.

I set out to write this book with three goals in mind. The first was to entertain just one reader. So if one reader's hair stood on end and felt a lion breathing down his neck, or if she cringed when envisioning a great white shark smashing his jaws just inches in front of her face, then I have succeeded.

The second goal was to impart the fragility and importance of family. If one family stays together after the loss of a loved one, or if one person finds the courage to face grief and leave behind guilt, then every drop of sweat that went into this book was worth it.

The final goal was to inspire just one reader to volunteer in whatever capacity he or she has, whether it's in their community, or across the globe. If just one person experiences the magic of giving, the world will swell with joy, and we will all be the better for the effort.

If you want to volunteer, start with your passion and see where it takes you. Maybe it will lead to saving gorillas in Uganda, cheetah in Botswana, great white sharks in South Africa, or providing leadership at your local Boys and Girls club. These are some of the organizations I have volunteered with and/or support.

www.edgeofafrica.com
www.bigfivevolunteer.com
www.theexpeditionproject.com
www.nourish.org.za
www.whitesharkafrica.com
www.pacificwhale.org
www.shark.org
www.cheetah.org
www.govolunteer.ca
www.davidsuzuki.org

Acknowledgements

This book would not have been made possible without the generous support and encouragement of so many amazing, wonderful people. I'd like to acknowledge a few of them here.

In Africa: Roger Wynn-Dyke of The Expedition Project, Dayne Davey of Edge of Africa, Kim and Hein at Umkhondo Big Five Volunteer Project, Melanie—my Kindred Spirit in South Africa, Ryan Roberts, The Drill Sergeant and Kittibon who had the tenacity to slap me every day until I finally woke up.

This book would have never been finished if it weren't for the unlimited support of some incredible friends. Juani and Cuchi, Judy, Betty, and Pilar—thank you for your wisdom and faith. To Paul; those three words are not enough.

Samantha, my big sis who is also my best friend, thank you. Will and Jack—my most attentive listeners at bedtime. CW, thank you for everything. William Landay, Best Selling Author, thank you for the direction.

To KM and HW, the support of life-long friends makes anything possible. To Anne Opotowsky, author and editor, thank you for your editing expertise. To Moksha Yoga, you brought stillness and clarity when I needed it. Namaste.

To the people who have brought this book to you, the reader, words can not express my eternal gratitude; Maryann Karinch of the Rudy Agency, whose patience goes unmatched, and Lynn Price, of Behler Publications; what an honor that you believed in me enough to publish my first book, thank you.

And finally to my mother and father who taught me the value of hard work and encouraged me to take chances. I love you, this book is for you.